THIS SWEATER IS FOR YOU!

SHELDON COHEN

afterword by **ROCH CARRIER**

THIS SWEATER

IS FOR YOU!

CELEBRATING THE CREATIVE PROCESS IN FILM AND ART
WITH THE ANIMATOR AND ILLUSTRATOR OF
"THE HOCKEY SWEATER"

ECW PRESS

Published by ECW Press
2120 Queen Street East, Suite 200, Toronto, Ontario, Canada M4E 1E2
416-694-3348 / info@ecwpress.com

Library and Archives Canada Cataloguing in Publication

Cohen, Sheldon, 1949-
This sweater is for you! : celebrating the creative process in film and art:
with the animator and illustrator of "The hockey sweater" / Sheldon Cohen.

1. Creation (Literary, artistic, etc.) in motion pictures. 2. Animated films--Canada.
I. Title. II. Title: The sweater.

N71.C64 2011   701'.15   C2011-902837-9

ISBN: 978-1-55022-960-8
also issued as:
978-1-77090-059-2 (PDF); 978-1-77090-058-5 (EPUB)

Editor: David Caron
Cover and Text Layout and Design: Ingrid Paulson
Production: Rachel Ironstone
Printing: Friesens   5   4   3   2   1

The publication of *This Sweater Is for You!* has been generously supported by
the Canada Council for the Arts which last year invested $20.1 million in writing
and publishing throughout Canada, and by the Ontario Arts Council, an agency
of the Government of Ontario. We also acknowledge the financial support of
the Government of Canada through the Canada Book Fund for our publishing
activities, and the contribution of the Government of Ontario through the Ontario
Book Publishing Tax Credit. The marketing of this book was made possible with
the support of the Ontario Media Development Corporation.

Printed and bound in Canada

CONTENTS

INTRODUCTION

THE OTHER DAY I was in the bank quietly doing my transactions when the teller noticed my name.

"Are you the Sheldon Cohen who does cartoons?"

"Well, sort of," I explained. "I make animated films and illustrate children's books, but there's actually another Sheldon Cohen in the city who draws cartoons. Weird, I know."

"Are you sure?" she asked again, half-hoping I'm wrong. "You weren't the one who taught my daughter how to make cartoons at summer camp?"

"No, that's the *other* Sheldon Cohen. I'm always getting calls to do birthday parties." Then I added as a joke, "My wife says I should take the jobs. No one'll ever know."

She gave a little courteous laugh and returned to her calculations. I could see she was disappointed.

"I did make a movie you probably heard of, though."

She peered up at me from her paperwork.

"It's called *The Sweater*."

"Sweater?"

"Maybe you know it as *The Hockey Sweater*? I also illustrated the children's book."

No reaction. By then I was getting desperate. "You know ... the one about Maurice Richard and the number 9 hockey sweater?"

"Sorry, no, I never heard of it."

AND SO, ONE of the people I'm writing this book for is my bank teller. But mainly it's for you, who, like millions of other viewers and readers, has come to treasure Roch Carrier's short story.

By the last line, we all feel it. There is something magical about this childhood tale. I never imagined that I would have had such a direct hand in touching that magic.

Recreating this great writer's vision through animation and illustration set me on an unforgettable journey. My art was the vehicle and the author's words, my road. I invite you to come along now as I take a look back at this rollicking ride.

A FEW WORDS before we embark.

Like all true adventures, I could not foresee the full landscape of this book until I actually set out recording the material. I originally intended that our journey would begin and end with *The Sweater*, but as the scope of my writing broadened, the starting point and final destination shifted considerably. Therefore, the travels ahead cover more ground than the making of a movie; they also include the making of an artist, and what began as a celebration of a classic Canadian short story ultimately became a celebration of the creative process itself.

Please climb aboard and join me as I retrace the highlights of a forty-year journey I truly never expected to take, beginning when I was not yet twenty years old.

186

Pre - SWEATER Years

1967
BY THE SKIN OF
MY TEETH

IT WAS TIME to pick a career. Fresh out of high school, I was asking myself the only real question a nice Jewish boy growing up in Montreal should be asking:

"Are my grades good enough to get into McGill University's dental school?"

Medicine seemed out of my league, but dentistry — that felt less daunting. And, of course, there was always orthodontics (if I really wanted to dream high). Regardless of my ultimate calling, I was thoroughly convinced that the sciences were for me.

The sciences, as it turned out, were thoroughly convinced otherwise. Physics, chemistry, biology — they nearly killed me. Even though I received that coveted Bachelor of Science degree after four grueling years at McGill, I knew I would never have a shiny brass nameplate outside a plush antiseptic-smelling office, engraved with the esteemed title, *Dr. Sheldon Cohen, DDS.*

Over the next few years, however, and to my great relief, I found myself steering away from root canals and into a vast new realm where I could truly thrive: the arts.

1970
HI-DIDDLE-DEE-DEE

I ALWAYS LOVED drawing. It came naturally to me; any skill carried over from my childhood was self-taught. I remember as a kid copying famous artwork from the *Books of Knowledge*, a popular household encyclopaedia sold door-to-door by travelling salesmen. They brought the treasures of past civilizations to our two-bedroom apartment on Van Horne Avenue. I was able to copy, for example, the *Mona Lisa*, a sixteenth-century painting created by the great Leonardo da Vinci. I read in one of the volumes that some historians believed it took the artist as long as fourteen years to complete his masterpiece.

And to think, I finished mine in twenty minutes (although, truth be told, my *Mona Lisa* looked more like Jack Benny).

Well!

With dental school now out of the picture, an unexpected floodgate opened up. My old love of drawing resurfaced like a forgotten friend. I didn't quite know how to greet it . . . until the day *Pinocchio* came to town.

The film was being re-released by Disney and I decided to ask a girl I knew if she wanted to see it.

That date was to change my life forever — not only because I ended up marrying that girl (a union ordained as soon as she agreed to see *Pinocchio*), but also because of something she whispered to me during the movie: "Do you realize we're watching a bunch of drawings? Isn't it fascinating?"

I looked back up at the screen. Right there and then it clicked! I knew what I would do with my art.

Nothing escaped my attention and some subjects were irresistible, as if calling out: "You must draw me."

Two portraits from that time stand out for me. One is of my mother, who, without really knowing it, understood the essence of art and the artist: honouring what is real and taking pure delight in it. There was not an ounce of vanity in her when those stack of curlers on top of her head called out: "You must draw me."

On the contrary, my incredibly beautiful grandmother — my father's mother — a very vain, wonderful woman, served as a glowing subject for another portrait that I framed for the walls of her apartment.

During one of my subsequent visits, I noticed her portrait out of the corner of my eye. Something about it caught my attention. No, it couldn't be!

"Bubbie, did you add lipstick to your picture?"

"Yeh," she said coyly in her thick Yiddish accent, "and a little rouge. I thought you made me look too pale."

God love this precious woman! She made it crystal clear that no artist in the world was going to play around with *her* reality.

1972
HIGHWAY 401

SUMMER WAS FAST approaching. I had now completed a full year at Sheridan College and returned to the same instructor with a fresh batch of drawings at the end of the semester. I was hoping to impress him with all the Fundamentals of Art I had learned.

"Sir, I have a request, if I may."

On my best behaviour, I explained that the Animation Department at the National Film Board of Canada was recruiting summer students in Montreal.

"I'm wondering if you could please put in a good word for me. It would really help to have a letter of recommendation from an animation teacher."

"Sorry," he said again, "there are other students I would send before you. Why don't you sign up for the full animation program next year and we'll take it from there."

I politely thanked him for his consideration, collected my drawings and . . . bought a bag of chips.

"Ah, the hell with him," I muttered to myself, wiping the salty crumbs from my face.

The following week I showed up at the NFB interview in Montreal with a very thin portfolio and no letter of recommendation (but wearing, if I might brag, a fine pair of personally handmade leather sandals).

I will be eternally grateful to Wolf Koenig, the executive producer in charge at the time. He didn't immediately turn me away as he very well could have, but said he saw something in my work. He told me to find a desk and think of a short film I'd like to animate over the summer.

My first big break!

I felt I had entered Animation Heaven where that Great Editor above could not have assembled a happier sequence of events for me. All I needed now was a soundtrack of angels singing in the background and the scene would have been complete.

15

I was stepping into a period at the NFB, often referred to as its "Golden Years," when Norman McLaren was directing dancers for his *Ballet Adagio*, Ryan Larkin was wrapping up his *Street Music*, and Caroline Leaf was raking grains of sand for her Inuit film.

You couldn't help bumping into award winners around every corner. Walking down the long corridors on the way to my desk, I'd peer into rooms and see Jacques Drouin creating landscapes on Pinscreen, Ishu Patel playing with beads under the camera, Co Hoedeman painting big wooden blocks for his stop-action *Tchou-Tchou*, and John Weldon, well, just being John Weldon — wildly funny, delivering something special as he animated his way towards the Oscars.

Alongside me, a growing number of newcomers were joining the NFB: Lynn Smith, Yossi Abolafia, Janet Perlman, Joyce Borenstein, Ellen Besen, and Veronika Soul.

In a strange way, I soon felt we were all part of a special family. It wasn't like now, when it seems that everyone and his brother is an animator. (Actually, my brother is a lawyer, but three of my cousins have since worked in animation.) Today most local schools and colleges offer Media Arts courses that teach anyone so inspired to create animated films on ordinary computers at home. Back then, however, we were a small community practising a unique craft. Each of us was intensely tied to our own projects, but we shared a common bond of excitement for everyone else's.

As for Sheridan College, I waved goodbye with my art diploma in hand and never looked back. It went on to become one of the finest animation schools in North America, specializing in classical training, while — unbeknownst to me — I would be remaining at the NFB, off and on, for the next three decades. At the time, however, there was no need to look very far ahead. My fortune was opening up right in front of me and I was ready to take on the world.

1973
STARTING WITH A JUMP

MY EARLIEST FILM was made using a pack of grease pencils, similar to crayons. I am referring to *Bossa Bop*, which ran a full two minutes and three seconds from beginning to end.

I like to think that I invented the first music video, long before MTV made this art form popular (even if mine was for the preschool set).

There was no rhyme or reason to the film, just three gangly characters choreographed to the beats and flow of an obscure soundtrack that I found in the NFB archives. Perky elevator music is what it sounded like, and yet for some reason, it jump-started my imagination.

I used its pulsating rhythm to experiment with the synchronization of picture and sound, as well as to understand the mechanics of movement.

How do I propel those three little characters through space? This was my first animation task, one that would eventually lead to a much bigger job of animating kids on a skating rink.

But for now, I was at the very beginning of a unique education for an animator. The National Film Board of Canada was offering me the best combination for innovative discovery: technical support for whatever film I wanted to make, with no preconceived ideas about what animation should be.

From where I sat in one of the little cubicles assigned to NFB summer students, I could see the clouds sailing past my window over a river of cars roaring below. Here, along the concrete expressway of the Metropolitan Boulevard, I was figuring out how to be a sorcerer. To my surprise, it was a sobering apprenticeship as I learned the cold, hard physics behind the magic.

1 second = 24 frames = 12 drawings (when double-framed).

Double-framing for standard movement.

Single-framing for smoother, more intricate movement.

Triple-framing for more limited movement.

Beware of strobing effects!

Avoid staggered action!

Ease in and ease out slowly!

Watch those increments!

20

Any true-blooded animator quickly becomes obsessed with an inescapable fixation on detail. But what really captivated me was the illusion itself: that first vivid moment of seeing the shapes and colours of my drawings radiate on screen. I was hooked! There was nothing I wanted to do more than to animate!

1974
ME AND ALFRED

I NEVER IMAGINED that those three dancing figures would rebound so quickly into another project. At the same time as *Bossa Bop* was wrapping up, the NFB Studio decided to produce an extensive series devoted to Canadian literature. It was called *Poets on Film,* designed as a compilation of short clips, and quite a number of them.

Therefore, newcomers like me were in a position to pitch fresh ideas to the Animation Department. There were hundreds, perhaps thousands, of poetry anthologies to choose from.

I had to take a deep breath. I asked myself: What process do I follow that will bring me to the *right* poem — the one that I ought to be working with?

And here is what I consider one of the most essential challenges for an artist. Amongst everything out there, how can we connect with what is meant for us?

In this particular case, it popped off the page, as simple as that! I saw the title of the poem and knew it was for me.

Death by Streetcar
by Raymond Souster

The old lady crushed to death by the Bathurst streetcar
had one cent left in her purse.
                         Which could mean only
one of two things: either she was wary of purse-snatchers
or all her money was gone.
                         If the latter,
she must have known her luck must very soon change,
for better or for worse:
                         which this day has decided.

It only took one reading. By the last line, the whole film had unfolded in my mind's eye: an arthritic character, hunched over with age, slowly putting on her coat as she prepares to leave her one-room apartment.

I would show the audience nothing more than this — just another morning in an old woman's life — except, when she leaves her house, it will be for the very last time. She has no idea of the streetcar waiting for her . . . but we do.

I got shivers. It was suspenseful, like a two-minute movie by Alfred Hitchcock (my favourite director).

The NFB liked my storyboard and signed me up to animate the film. I was sent to Toronto where I could meet the poet in person and discuss the project.

"Why that one? I have another poem. It's much better for animation." Raymond Souster tried to convince me to read some verses he wrote about a spider. "It's a natural for children."

It didn't matter, though. I was learning something that all artists must learn, and it went far beyond the study of technique. I was approaching the very core of creativity — that fertile ground where the birth takes place, in a thought, an idea, a vision. Only the creator has that first flicker of its life and, ultimately, can choose to stand by it — or not. That is why I could say to Raymond Souster, "I'm sure."

To clarify, it wasn't stubbornness on my part; it was a simple "knowing" and a decision to honour what I knew.

From that early time on, the way was clear: the only reliability one can abide by is an inner compass, and the only direction one can trust is from the inside out.

For this reason, like all artists working out of a void, I am constantly listening within in order to stay on course.

Not wanting to appear rude, I politely resisted.

"Sorry," I told him, "I'm not really interested in that one."

"You're sure about 'Death by Streetcar'?"

"I'm sure."

How could I blame him? A film with "Death" and "Streetcar" in the same title — there could be nothing cute about this cartoon.

1976
IN-BETWEEN JOBS

I'M LIVING IN New York City now. How did this happen? I have to thank *Death by Streetcar*. Although the film didn't win any prizes at the Ottawa International Film Festival, just the fact that it was accepted for competition gave me enough clout to have landed a job in the Big Apple.

It's my first day. I'm sitting at my desk waiting for instructions.

"Raggedy Ann and Andy. One moooo-ment please."
"Raggedy Ann and Andy. One moooo-ment please."
"Raggedy Ann and Andy. One moooo-ment please."

The receptionist's throaty mantra drones on in the background as she puts a continuous stream of callers on hold. She's a tough, stocky, bleached-blonde New Yorker whose gravelly vocal cords, I imagine, have been worn down by years of cigarettes and alcohol.

We're way up high in a midtown Manhattan skyscraper, the whole floor devoted to a multi-million-dollar animated feature gearing into full production. A little tin bell suddenly dings frantically from the marbled hallway and throws me out of my trance. It's not a fire alarm because the others around me are walking calmly out the door. I join the civilized line that has formed in front of a mobile snack cart offering beverages, pastries, and pre-packaged sandwiches. I haven't yet received my assignment and I'm already on my first official coffee break.

It hasn't quite sunk in. I'm actually here in New York City with a job, a working visa, and a place of my own. Out of the three, the most difficult, by far, has been finding an apartment. I grabbed it as soon as the landlady's squinting face peered out from behind the thin crack of her basement door, eyeing me suspiciously but finally deciding it was okay to make the offer. "There's one flat upstairs; it's not very big."

Sheer joy! I finally have a miserably depressing pipe-clanking one-bedroom third-floor walk-up—but it's mine, and my great odyssey through the classifieds is over.

The ten minutes of our unionized coffee break brings everyone promptly back to our desks. I'm thinking of my apartment now as I slowly re-wrap the cellophane around the giant cheese Danish I couldn't finish. Since moving to this city, I'm much more careful with crumbs, my cockroach sensitivity on high alert. The one last night, it just wouldn't

die. Me with my Buddhist's inclinations—I became a madman, smashing that segmented intruder over and over again with the sole of my running shoe. And still it marched along the grease-stained linoleum floor, oblivious, invincible. What kind of monster lives with me and how many more will suddenly appear tonight under the stark white glare of the single light bulb dangling from my kitchen ceiling?

"Well, I see you're all set up and ready to go." My anxiety is suddenly interrupted by the energetic animation supervisor, Michael Sporn (who, many years later, will go on to become head of his own highly successful studio). He plops a huge folder onto my desk, brimming with at least twenty-five large sheets of animation paper.

"Try this scene. I'll come by later in the day and see how you're doing. If you have questions about the *in-betweens*, just ask anyone around you."

"Will do." I nod back with enough confidence to make him feel this really isn't the biggest mistake he has ever made, inviting me to come all the way from Canada.

He continues down the aisle, moving methodically from station to station, distributing more cream-coloured folders as he goes. Each one contains a different sequence inscribed with cryptic messages (or so it appears to the untrained eye), explaining exactly how the top animation brass — including, among others, Richard Williams, Gerald Potterton, Art Babbitt, and Tissa David — have instructed us to bring Raggedy Ann and her brother, Andy, to life.

I turn to the young person busy at work beside me, one of many in this animation factory. The room is arranged in a giant grid of pre-fabricated, pressed-wood desks newly equipped with thick metal discs on top of the table and custom-fitted lightboxes underneath.

From what I can tell, we've been grouped according to a hierarchy of importance, the co-workers around me sharing the bottom rung.

"Excuse me."

My neighbour looks up. I've disturbed him from some intricate paper-flipping activity that has been absorbing his full attention. Still, he seems friendly. There's a spark of recognition: "Oh, you're the guy from the National Film Board of Canada."

"That's me."

"They make amazing films. I really respect that place."

I see that I've impressed him just by association. "It is pretty great there," I concur, and then can't help adding, "Sometimes Norman McLaren has lunch with us in the cafeteria."

Not having done much in the industry, this is the biggest claim to fame I can muster. I get back to the point. "I'm just wondering, what exactly are *in-betweens*?"

The look on his face — the utter disbelief — once he realizes I'm not joking! But if there was a joke to tell, it would go something like this:

"Knock, knock."

"Who's there?"

"Ben."

"Ben who?"

"Ben a real fluke that I was hired to work on Raggedy Ann and Andy and have no idea what 'in-betweens' are!"

Thanks to the discretion of my very qualified in-betweening neighbour, I was able to avoid any humiliating deportation. He provided a crash course on the paper-flipping skills I so desperately lacked. Dexterity and visual acuity — that's what it takes to do this job.

The in-betweener fits Drawing A onto what they call a *peg bar*, adding Drawing C on top, and then covering both with a blank sheet that will become Drawing B.

Then Drawings A and C are flipped back and forth as the in-betweener watches the movement from one position to the next, while at the same time sketching the "in-between" action on Drawing B—hence the name of this convoluted technique.

Aside from figuring out how to flip all three sheets in the right order (in my particular case, my poor uncoordinated fingers could barely follow the messages from my brain!), the most difficult part is to keep watching the movement between Drawings A and C as Drawing B is taking shape. (Again, my poor uncoordinated eyes were having the same problem as my fingers.)

The pressure never lets up. The pencil lines created on Drawing B must be perfectly seamless in matching up with Drawings A and C to avoid any distractions when the animation ultimately ends up on screen.

When this entire process suddenly clicks into place (as it eventually does), there is a euphoric feeling of accomplishment and a great rejoicing of hand-eye coordination! But until that point, how does the in-betweener feel? . . .

Like Goofy, Clumsy Smurf, Homer Simpson—d'oh! Take your pick!

I blame that hard-nosed instructor at Sheridan College for denying me this vital skill every commercial animator must acquire. Had he been a bit more gracious with my application, I would surely have been able to join the marketplace with a full basket of first-year basics: flipbooks, bouncing ball exercises, and lip-synching. What a crime! I never learned to "squash and stretch" my characters with the best of them, that son of a . . .

Just joking—I'm actually happy he didn't let me into the course. It forced me to join the animation world on my own primitive terms, using whatever raw talent I possessed. *Primitive* and *raw*—the personal trademarks that would soon be stamping my signature style onto a film about a boy and his worn-out hockey sweater.

After a year in New York, however, I had no idea this project was waiting for me back in Canada. Perhaps my little detour was all for the best because in spite of lagging behind, I would now be able to approach this new job fully prepared with the obscure art of in-betweening.

Animating
THE SWEATER
1978-80

MY SECOND BIG BREAK

IT IS A ten-minute trip from producer Marrin Canell's house to his place of work at the National Film Board of Canada in Montreal. In that short period of time, he hears something on his car radio that captivates his attention during the entire ride in.

Up on the third floor, in the same sprawling building for which Marrin is headed, I am clearing off my desk, about to start a new project. It is a thirty-second clip from the "Canada Vignette" series being produced by the NFB. I feel lucky that the Animation Department kept the door open after my brief stint on *Raggedy Ann and Andy*. It didn't take me long to change my New York state of mind and pursue a less commercial approach to making films. It's very clear to me now. I am much more suited for personally-inspired projects such as those encouraged at the NFB.

As I sit there, deep in thought, I try to figure out how to fill in the tiny boxes of my storyboard. This image . . . or that one?

"Excuse me, Sheldon."

I look up and see it's Marrin.

"I heard something on the radio coming into work today. I'd like you to listen to it."

IF I COULD freeze-frame the one defining moment in my career that influenced everything that came after (including the publication of this memoir over thirty years later), it was exactly then — when Marrin came by my desk that sunny morning in the spring of 1978.

The broadcast he was referring to — which had just played across Canada on CBC radio — was narrated by Roch Carrier. As a rising star on the Quebec literary scene, he had been asked to write a radio piece discussing the tensions between French and English cultures in Canada.

"What does Quebec want?" That was the actual question posed to the author. Later I found out that Roch's immediate response was "How do you answer that?"

Anything he tried to write felt too dry, too uninteresting. Then he flashed on an incident from his childhood in the tiny village of Sainte-Justine, Quebec. He jotted down the story and decided it would be a much better way to explain to English Canada the life and aspirations of the French-speaking communities he knew best.

Thus was born *The Sweater* (later known as *The Hockey Sweater* when published as a book). It never occurred to the author that he was delivering to the rest of Canada what was to become one of the country's most cherished tales of all time.

A few days later, I listened to the recording that Marrin retrieved from CBC. He played it straight through from beginning to end. I was still smiling from that now-familiar last line of the story when Marrin closed the tape machine and looked at me with that self-assured, solid expression that all great producers have. His demeanour could not have been more earnest. He knew he had a treasure in his hands.

"This *has* to be an animated film! It's all there."

He explained to me how a number of directors (more experienced than me) were busy on other projects and turned down the story. Wolf Koenig — the same person who gave me my first big break — had made a suggestion to Marrin, "What about Sheldon?"

"Me?" I thought. Could I really do justice to this thoroughly French-Canadian story about life in a Catholic village? I'm English-speaking, from a big city, not a great hockey player and, being Jewish (which explains why I wasn't a great hockey player), I had very little experience with the Church.

"Will you give it a shot?" asked Marrin.

I really didn't know if I was the right one for this job, but there it was in front of me:

"Sure, I'll see what I can do."

It didn't seem momentous at the time. In fact, I wasn't even certain I'd be hired in the end. Roch Carrier still had to agree to bring me on board.

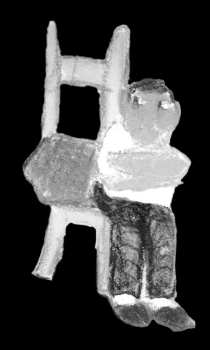

Marrin arranged for me to show a sample of my artwork to the author in a meeting set up the following week. To prepare, I tried my best to draw my version of Roch's mother holding up the sweater. But when it came time to present it, I thought it was much too primitive. Why didn't I work on it more?

And what about young Roch sitting on the chair! Oh my God, what was I thinking? I made him look like a little old man!

Roch's face lit up when he saw what I drew. "Yes, that's it! That's exactly the feeling!"

I was thrilled. The job was mine!

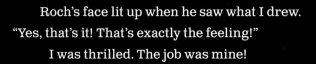

A TRIP TO
THE COUNTRY

LIKE MOST ENGLISH Quebecers in the 1950s, I loved watching the Plouffe Family as much as I loved watching the Ricardos.

But if I was to do this film justice, I would require a great deal more information about life in a French-Canadian home than that provided by a TV set. The Internet didn't exist yet, but it didn't matter. I had something much better: Roch Carrier! He personally escorted me to his village of Sainte-Justine.

we landed in Quebec City after a forty-five-minute flight from Montreal. "My village is near the U.S. border," Roch told me as we headed south in a rented car.

Roch's hand

I began collecting as many images as I could:

barns and fields...

...and more barns and fields...

...all along beautiful winding roads.

37

I loved being in the country!

I remember Roch saying that every time he came back here from the city he could actually hear the trees singing.

After about an hour, Roch used the windshield wipers to clear away the mounting number of bugs stuck on the glass. He pointed his finger towards the horizon.

"Do you see the steeple way in the distance?"

I couldn't say that I did. Wait.

I see it !

Roch beamed. "Every village in the Quebec country-side announces itself in this way."

I could tell he was proud.

"Welcome to my childhood home!"

I was excited! We were entering the Land of The Sweater!

INSIDE THE VILLAGE

MY VISIT BEGAN with the biggest greeting of all!

It came from a towering presence that watched over everyone for miles around...in their houses, on the streets and across the fields to the outlying farms.

Roch explained that religion was at the core of every aspect of village life. Looking up at the statue with its outstretched arms, even I couldn't avoid the all-pervading force of the Church. To its faithful followers, I understood how it was a source of love — and to those who strayed, how it could readily turn into a source of fear. I realized the film would have to begin this way — with the statue standing tall at the entrance to this tiny, isolated Quebec community — a central figure reflecting the utter prominence of the Catholic Church.

A little bit of trivia
from a would-be
dentist...

Flicking white paint off a
toothbrush gives a perfect
snowflake effect.

42

43

BEGINNING WITH THE ENDING

MY EDUCATION WAS now officially underway.

Stop Number One: a peek inside the church.

Everything in the story of *The Sweater* eventually leads right back to these doors.

A FEW DECADES before my visit, ten-year-old Roch climbed the very steps I was about to take, but, of course, at that time he wore a certain sweater — one that, as the author wrote, "weighed on my shoulders like a mountain." But that's for later.

As soon as we passed through the hallowed archway, the outside world ceased to exist. Peace and solitude met the visitor inside the stillness of these stone walls, and I understood at once why the villagers felt that here was a place you could talk to God.

Gazing past the rafters and into the mysterious darkness above, my mind envisioned sleeping moths wedged behind the old wooden beams, ready to be conjured into flight by the imagination of a young child.

The scene in *The Sweater* that features the church ceiling contains the only 'background' in the film that I didn't paint myself. Although I had a hand in its design, when it came time to actually colour it, I felt I couldn't do it justice and asked NFB animator and artist Bob Doucet to render it. As soon as I watched the beauty of his watercolours fill up the scene, I realized what a good move it had been to hand the paintbrush over to him. His mastery of the technique lent itself perfectly to the atmosphere needed at the end of the film.

But enough of final scenes. I was only at the very start of my research.

THE TOUR CONTINUES

BACK IN THE open air, Roch pointed to a neighbouring farm.

"See that big dry patch of grass?"

I nodded yes. Being a city boy, I was fascinated with the giant black and white cow standing there. Could I pet it, I wondered?

"You're looking at where our skating rink was!"

Roch explained how every winter one of the villagers nailed old wooden boards together around a large surface of ice for the children to play hockey.

"But when spring returned," he continued, "the cows reclaimed their pasture until the next winter season. April was not a happy time for me and my friends."

What Roch had just described would later become the opening scene for a children's book, entitled *The Boxing Champion*. Little did I know I would be painting number 9s for many years to come!

47

48

A DRIVE DOWN MAIN STREET

IN FRENCH IT's called "rue principale" — a quaint thorough-fare lined with little wooden houses, one after the other.

The future would eventually bring shopping plazas and chain stores to the region but I was lucky enough to be there when I could still have a glimpse into the past.

And there it was: the General Store — the place where Roch's mother was "too proud" to buy his clothes!

Part of my job was to imagine how everything must have looked, not only covered in snow, but also some thirty years earlier when Roch was a child.

Looking back at this particular scene, I wonder how I could have mixed up one of the first French words I learned in elementary school. It was part of the vocabulary our teacher drilled into us over and over again.

"Répétez, la classe. The store . . . le magasin."

So imagine my surprise when a French-speaking colleague pointed out that the sign in my painting had an extra *E* at the end of the word "general." Of course he was right. "Le magasin . . . le magasin . . . not la magasin." All those repetition exercises and still I got it wrong.

When I told Roch about my mistake, he laughed and said, "Yes, I saw that you wrote it incorrectly, but I thought you did it on purpose."

He explained that many of the older people in his village didn't have the opportunity to attend school and, therefore, it was not uncommon to see misspellings just like that. Nevertheless, thinking of how my third-grade teacher would have scowled at this simple mistake, I quickly painted over the *E* so that I could film the scene again with the proper spelling.

BACK TO THE tour of Sainte-Justine...

We continued our drive along Rue Principale. Roch unexpectedly veered the car into the parking lot of the neighbourhood restaurant.

"I can't come back to my village without stopping here," he said with a big smile. "You're in for a very special treat!"

I was ready for a good cup of coffee from the local *casse-croûte* (the Quebec version of a diner).

What came with it, though, I was not prepared for — fresh homemade sugar pie! One bite and I instantly felt the intensity of the sugar hitting my bloodstream.

With our eyes glazed over, Roch and I continued happily towards our destination.

MEETING ROCH'S MOTHER

JUST DOWN THE street, we came to the last stop on our tour. "Here we are. This is the house."

Roch's mother greeted us in the big family kitchen. I sensed a warmth and wisdom in her sparkling blue eyes and made a mental note to capture this quality for the animation. After all, this was not just Roch's mother I was meeting. She was his "supporting actress," the second leading role in the film.

And then Roch said, "Wait here. I have something to show you."

He returned carrying a large, rectangular antique, and placed it carefully on the kitchen table.

"This is the radio we all sat around every Saturday night. The whole family would listen to our hockey team fight it out."

An entire era seemed to be contained inside this big wooden box. I made another note to include this image in the opening of the film.

With the collection of all these details, the stage was set for Roch to pass the creative torch to me. The author's childhood was now officially in my hands.

"Use my words as a springboard," Roch said at the end of our trip, and with this generous blessing, we parted ways for nearly two years, leaving me and my art to tell his story.

LEFT TO
THE IMAGINATION

Les hivers de mon enfance
étaient des saisons longues, longues.
Nous vivions en trois lieux:
l'école, l'église et la patinoire; mais
la vraie vie était sur la patinoire.
Roch Carrier

The winters of my childhood were
long, long seasons. We lived in
three places – the school, the church
and the skating-rink – but our real life
was on the skating-rink.

THERE IS A good chance that the words highlighted on the previous page are neatly folded inside the wallet of the average Canadian. These opening lines from *The Hockey Sweater* have been inscribed on our recently re-designed five-dollar bill.

When David Verrall, co-producer of *The Sweater*, heard that an excerpt from Roch Carrier's short story was being commemorated in this way, he was delighted. It meant that the NFB animated film would be part of a very special legacy.

I didn't quite know how to tell him. The person in the Royal Canadian Mint who has the job of choosing quotations that go onto money had selected the only text from the author's story that *isn't* in the film.

I SUPPOSE I'M to blame. Those specific words ended up on the editing-room floor when I cut the voice track many years before. There was a simple reason why. It wasn't words that began the film for me; it was a series of images.

FORM OUT OF FORMLESSNESS

IT IS SAID that all life emerges from an infinite void. In the Quebec countryside, when it's winter, the void is a vast whiteness. Solid shapes appear and disappear from behind blowing snowdrifts.

I added darker and darker oil pastels to the background, bringing night with the sled's arrival.

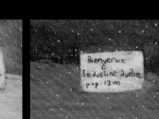

However, as the film begins, it is not just any night — it's *Saturday* night, when everyone in the little village listens to the Montreal Canadiens hockey game on the radio. I imagined that even the resident priest would cut his prayers short so as not to miss the opening face-off.

A LITTLE SIDE note about this scene . . .

Someone hesitantly mentioned to me that the priest should have crossed himself with his right hand, not his left, as I had animated it. Unfortunately, the film was already in distribution when this was brought to my attention and I was not able to make any changes. Hence, the movie will forever remain with a left-handed priest (drawn by myself, a left-handed animator — perhaps reason enough to explain this slight transgression).

A PASSION FOR "THE ROCKET"

"BURNING ENTHUSIASM." THAT'S how the author describes the adulation he and his friends felt for Maurice Richard, the greatest hockey hero of the time.

No other sports figure in Quebec history has come close to generating the passion that this "Idol of a People" did during his celebrated career with the Montreal Canadiens, beginning in 1942 until his retirement in 1960. Game after game, he raced down the ice with a blazing force that made him the one and only "Rocket" to millions of beloved fans!

I did my best to bring out the fiery gaze you see in all the photos from that era.

In order to capture the Rocket's intensity, I paid special attention to getting the expression of his eyes exactly right.

Long after his number 9 was retired, I met Maurice Richard at a couple of promotional events.

1980 MONTREAL FORUM

Marvin Canell Producer | David Verrall Producer | That's me | Roch Carrier | THE ROCKET | Derek Lamb Executive Producer

Even though he was much older, and his demeanour mellower than at the height of his career, you could still sense the same fire behind his eyes.

Maurice Richard's connection with *The Sweater* was mainly through the author, and there wasn't much talk between the Rocket and me. However, I remember one time sitting beside him at a book-signing event with hundreds of people lined up to meet this great legend. I was in a kind of daze, adding my signature to book after book, and passing each copy on to the Rocket, the one everyone was really waiting for. I felt a bit out of place in all the eagerness of these fervent hockey fans. At one point the Rocket leaned over. "You really sign your name quickly," he said.

There was something very human about hearing Rocket Richard — the greatest of greats and a god to so many — quietly tell me this. He was just a decent, unassuming person.

Then he went back to signing his own autograph for the ecstatic fan waiting patiently for this treasured souvenir.

He slowly formed one letter after another, exercising the utmost precision over each character. And the result was a collector's dream come true: a "Maurice Richard" signature written with that same deliberate intensity with which he did everything else.

"We were five Maurice Richards against five other Maurice Richards, throwing themselves on the puck."

-Excerpt from Roch Carrier's narration of *The Sweater*

65

A MAGIC SHOW

THE SUN WOULD come up each morning and I couldn't wait to get to the NFB studio. In what other job do you start your work watching entire worlds flash into existence? During daily "rushes" of *The Sweater,* the technician would play back the most recent footage developed in the lab the night before. Each new scene brought its own thrill as I saw my animated characters fill the wall-to-wall movie screen in the pitch-black theatre.

And to think, every bit of the sweeping action that ended up being projected—like the skating sequence on the opposite page—was all drawn within an area that measured no more than 8″×6″. (This was the average "field size" for most of the artwork in the movie.)

When you see the animation on screen, the characters appear to be advancing through great expanses of 3-D space, far into the distance, but, of course, it is all deception. I drew each skater in smaller and smaller proportions against a tiny fixed flat background. Et voilà! The boys end up at the rink, seemingly hundreds of feet away.

Roch told me that when it came time to play hockey with his friends, he would lace up his skates at home and leave in full gear right from his kitchen door. Therefore, I wanted you, as the viewer, to see what would look like a steady flow of bright red Canadiens sweaters streaming through the frozen village streets.

Again, you are being fooled. You think you are watching continuous movement, but it's an illusion. A movie is nothing more than individual pictures, strung together frame by frame.

For the trick to work, however, the animator must rely on the speed of technology. The images on screen flash by your eyes — as fast as the Rocket himself. In fact, they race by so quickly that your brain fills in the missing gaps automatically. The scientific term for this neural process is *persistence of vision*.

I just call it magic.

DID I MENTION THAT ANIMATION IS INSANE?

Disclaimer: The following material contains graphic content not intended for aspiring animation students. The author does not accept responsibility for any sudden change of career or future AA memberships.

PEOPLE ARE SURPRISED when I tell them that it took two years to make a ten-minute film. They are even more surprised when I tell them how many drawings went into the animation of *The Sweater*. If you're thinking in the hundreds, keep going. Don't stop at five thousand. The answer: just over *ten thousand* drawings.

I can't say it enough: animation is insane! There is probably no other profession that is more nitpicky and tedious. Each fraction of a second has to be visually created and manipulated, frame by frame, before it goes on screen.

Perhaps that's why I would hear people in the business say that animators are near the top of the list of "Most Likely to Be Alcoholics." It never bothered me, though. In my case, I felt I dodged a bullet. We all know who's said to be at the top of the list of "Most Likely to Commit Suicide." That's right: dentists!

Coming on board an animated production is like entering a time warp. For instance, when planning the scene of Roch's mother ordering his new hockey sweater, I thought to myself, "Why don't I have the kid run into frame while his mother's writing the letter? He looks over her shoulder and then runs off. No, wait . . . first a bubble appears and he imagines himself wearing the sweater. Maybe he shows it off to his friends. Then the bubble disappears and he runs off-screen as the mother looks up."

Total time to come up with that idea: ten seconds.

Total time to animate it: ten *weeks*.

Let me explain how this little brainstorm of an idea translated into an over two month flurry of intensive teamwork.

The preparation for that particular sequence of scenes included painting all the settings as fully rendered art-work ("backgrounds") based on preliminary planned-out action ("layouts"); drawing the main positions of the char-acters ("keys") as quick sketches ("roughs"); filming the drawings with a 16mm camera ("pencil testing"); tracing the rough keys so that they were neatly rendered into pre-cise drawings ("clean-ups"); filling in the middle positions ("in-betweening" — as you know, my personal nemesis), fol-lowed by more testing; then re-tracing the full batch of clean-ups onto celluloid sheets ("cels") and colouring them with special acrylics ("inking and painting"); and finally, filming the thousands of hand-painted cels using a 35mm Oxberry camera stand ("final shooting").

Next came the editing, where the picture was spliced together and the frames nipped and tucked to avoid irritat-ing transitions ("jump-cuts"). Then came the synchronization of the audio track (music, sound effects, and voices), matching it with the picture track, which was originally filmed as a storyboard reel ("animatic") and gradually became the finished product after each story-board panel was replaced with the corresponding final animation.

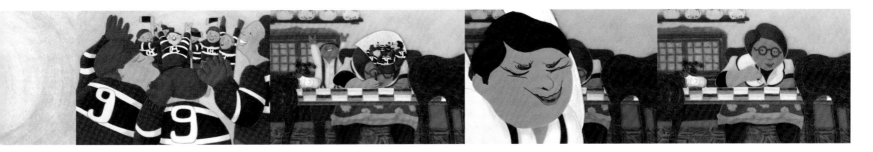

I don't know your reaction after reading this, but I am consumed with anxiety just having listed all these details. Clearly *animation is insane*!

Because of the inordinate length of time required to make an animated film, every idea must be vetted carefully before committing to it. Will it work or won't it? There were times when the cleaning staff would empty overflowing garbage bins from my office filled with test after test of animation gone bad. I learned the hard way that it was far more important to know what to discard right from the beginning than to follow through on work that I was not one hundred percent certain was worth developing.

It is no easy task we undertake, breathing life into drawings. That is the difference between animation and other art forms. Nothing is ever static in the illusory world the animator creates. Keep in mind that every single bit of action that moves on screen is *artificial*, the origin of this word describing perfectly our job at hand: "made by man," and, might I add, by women too — although, like most professions, animation was late in inviting the other half to join its crazy ways.

tain a semblance of reality — in this case, something as simple as snow falling outside the window.

Let me correct that. I used the word "simple" to describe the snow falling, but when it comes to the art of animation, nothing is actually simple. It took many days for me to create that little bit of weather. Every single flake required its own line of action, advancing in the tiniest of increments, a fraction of an inch for each new position.

All together now... ANIMATION IS INSANE!

FROM A CHILD'S PERSPECTIVE

I OFTEN USE exaggerated angles to show a character's point of view, especially when it is that of a child who is always looking up at the world.

For instance, in the post office scene, I drew little Roch reaching way up high to send his mother's letter off to Monsieur Eaton.

Speaking of Monsieur Eaton, I am reminded of a note I received from a young student who told me how much he liked the film, but added:

"Do you realize that you made a mistake? Mr. Eaton is English and you wrote *Monsieur* Eaton on his nameplate."

I was very impressed by this student's keen sense of observation. Today, he must be close to forty years old since I received his letter almost thirty years ago. Judging from his analytical skills, I wouldn't be surprised if he has become a very successful litigator.

However, I ought to explain that I did make a deliberate choice in the way I wrote the nameplate. The setting of this scene, unlike the real department store, is meant to be a fantasy inside the imagination of young Roch, who would only know the grand owner of the catalogue company the way his mother always referred to him . . . as *Monsieur* Eaton, not Mr. Eaton.

Phew, I rest my case.

MONSIEUR EATON

IN THIS SCENE, Roch's family gleefully opens the package that Monsieur Eaton has sent.

It is here where the tension of the story is at its highest.

I use the word "tension" in order to best convey the emotional hold the film has on you, the viewer, at this point.

Everything in the first half of the story — the joy, the dreams, the anticipation of a new sweater — has served as a build-up for the unexpected "fall" in the second half.

In fact, the word *anticipation* is a technical term used to describe a basic rule adhered to by animators: In order to create natural-looking movement, the opposite action must precede the start of the main action.

For example, if I want to have a character take a slap shot with a hockey stick, I must animate the stick moving backwards first in order to put real force behind the subsequent forward action.

It is the same with storytelling. For us to feel "one of the greatest disappointments" of Roch Carrier's life, we need to be filled with the young boy's glorious vision of the "red, white, and blue costume of the Montreal Canadiens, the best team in the world!" That way, the utter blow of receiving "the blue and white sweater of the Toronto Maple Leafs" will have the strongest impact.

And perhaps it is the same with growing up. For children to find their own sense of empowerment, they need to contend with their sense of utter powerlessness in an adult world.

I had great fun animating the cat-and-mouse interaction where Roch's mother traps the desperate child trying to escape from this nightmare! It's the closest I'll ever come to a Tom and Jerry moment in my work. It remains one of my favourite scenes in the film: Roch circling wildly around the wood stove, scampering across that old-fashioned linoleum floor.

Roch explained to me that the kitchen was the centre of family activity in a French-Canadian home — often the biggest room in the house and the one a person enters first from the outside. I kept that in mind when I planned the settings for many of the interior shots.

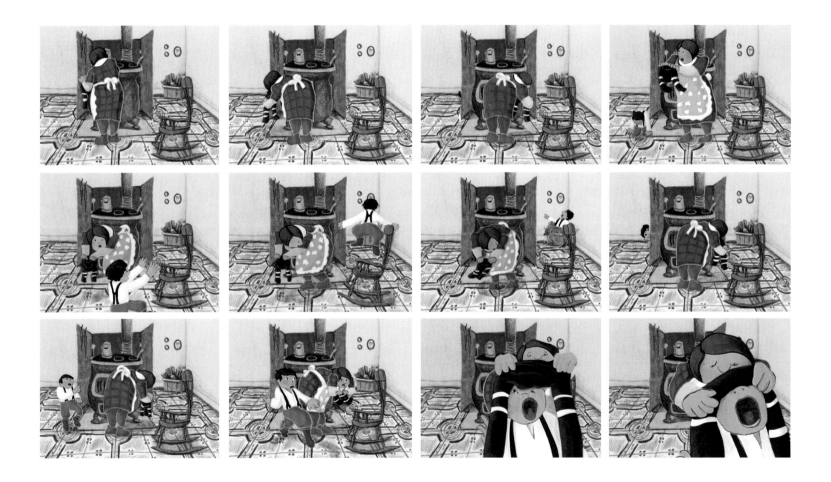

MOVIE SCRIPT FOR THE CHASE SCENE:

ROCH:

"I'll never wear that uniform!"

MOTHER:

"First of all, you're going to try it on. If you make up your
mind about something before you try it, my boy, you won't
go very far in this life."

ROCH:

"I can't wear that!"

MOTHER:

"Why? This sweater is a perfect fit."

ROCH:

"Maurice Richard would never wear it."

MOTHER:

"You're not Maurice Richard. Besides, it's not what you put on
your back that matters, it's what you put inside your head."

ROCH:

"You'll never make me put in my head to wear a Toronto
Maple Leafs sweater."

LOSING OUR "USUAL POSITION"

"A BIG SMILE for the camera, Roch!"

I imagine these were the instructions that the reluctant subject must have heard just before this photo was snapped.

Yes, *The Sweater* is a true story, as evidenced by that big, white emblem of the Toronto Maple Leafs, smack dab in the middle of the young hockey player's chest — a spot until then proudly reserved for the "C H" of the Montreal Canadiens.

He managed to smile for the camera, but I wonder if this photo was taken just before he ventures to the rink for the very first time in his brand new sweater. If so, we know his smile will very soon be disappearing.

Poor kid!

Roch Ste. Justine 1946

IN MAKING AN animated film, every scene has to be planned with the utmost care. A detailed series of little boxes, compiled into a *storyboard*, lays out the visuals of each sequence with accompanying text, and keeps the director on track throughout production.

Animators follow the storyboard so religiously that it is often referred to as "the Bible."

FOR EACH SCENE in *The Sweater*, I wanted to make sure that you would be getting the full impact of the story through my visuals. Therefore, I considered designing every layout in the strongest way possible.

FULL CIRCLE

ANIMATED MOVEMENT WILL feel stunted if a fundamental rule is not followed: When going from Point A to Point B, it is better to create a curved path rather than one that proceeds along a straight line. By tracing a somewhat arc-shaped route, these *lines of action* produce a more satisfying sense of movement for the viewer.

As it turned out, I soon discovered that I was only partway along my own creative arc in terms of collaborating with Roch Carrier. At the end of *The Sweater*, neither of us was aware of a whole series of children's books waiting down the road.

But for now, after years of devoted work on the film, I felt a deep sense of accomplishment. My job was done. As I packed up the piles and piles of artwork on the floor around my desk, I thought back to the first day of production, pencil in hand, poised and ready to go. The floor was empty then, but I sensed it. There was an excitement in the air. Something good was about to fill up in this room.

Post-SWEATER Years

"You're only as good as your last film."

. . . . so they say

1982
WHO KNEW THERE WAS SUCH A WORD AS "SCATOLOGICAL"?

THE RESPONSE WAS instant. *The Sweater* hit its mark right from its initial launch. The film soared through the festival circuit, collecting awards from all parts of Canada and the U.S., and even from England where it received the prestigious BAFTA for Best Animated Film, an honour equal to the Oscar in America and granted under the patronage of the Queen's daughter, Princess Anne.

And so, finding myself in the company of royalty, I perched myself on a pedestal with my head held high enough to see the top shelf of my bookcase — the perfect place to line up all my prizes in a row. It was surprisingly easy! You make a film, send it out there, and then just sit back as the awards roll in.

I could hardly wait to use my art again to adapt more stories into film. Soon after I finished *The Sweater*, Caroline Leaf (one of animation's leading filmmakers) asked me to consider a project that she was producing for the National Film Board of Canada. I jumped at the chance.

"There are a few stories you can choose from," she said, showing me a pile of anthologies she had collected.

"Here's one about an older woman at the end of her life. Or how about this one, from the Prairies, about two neighbours who argue over a cow, or —"

"Did you say cow?" I stopped her mid-sentence. "I love cows. That's the one for me."

Contented as the creature I was about to animate, I soon found myself directing and animating a new film called *Pies*. There was no reason to think its success would be any different this time around. In fact, when I first called the author, Wilma Riley, to ask if I could adapt her short story into an animated movie, she was stunned.

"This is incredible!" I heard her voice bursting through the phone receiver all the way from Saskatchewan. "I know *The Sweater*. After I saw that film, I had a secret wish that you would animate one of my stories! I can't believe you are calling me about *Pies*!"

"It's meant to be!" I thought to myself, cementing what I already believed — that, as Roch Carrier would say, my moment had come!

Even the NFB was accommodating its bright new star with a bigger office, talented assistants, and all the animation cel paint I needed to carry on with my latest vision. Everything was on track and I forged ahead, happy as an animator could be.

Wham! Right into a brick wall!!!

It was the brown cel paint that did me in.

If I may explain...

The title, *Pies*, is a play on words referring to both meat pies and cow pies, the latter, of course, being a euphemism for cow manure. Hence, I required many jars of brown cel paint to render this Prairies story.

Pies is set in the early 1950s on the outskirts of Regina, where city meets farm. Immigrants from war-torn Europe are beginning to create new lives in Canada, but many are unable to leave behind their old hatreds. The movie is about two such women: a refined German *hausfrau* and her earthier Polish neighbour, who owns a cow.

The presence of this enormous manure-producing farm animal sparks an explosive exchange of racial slurs between the two ladies, which escalates into a barrage of hand-thrown cow pies. I never imagined my training as an artist, limited as it was, would one day serve as preparation for animating globs of dung flying through the air.

Ha Ha – Who's dirty now?

You pig woman!
You dirty pig.

Original storyboard, pg. 8
from NFB film 'PIES'.

Pies is a nasty tale, indeed, with the juiciest part to be savoured at the end. Intent on revenge, the German lady scoops a spoonful of bovine droppings into the ingredients of a meat pie and deviously serves the freshly baked good to her unsuspecting Polish adversary, all under the guise of neighbourly friendship.

Author Wilma Riley provides an unexpected twist to the ending of her story and sweetens the bitter quarrel between the two women with a heartfelt resolution.

UPON THE MOVIE's release, I quickly learned that the subject matter of *Pies* was upsetting quite a number people. A scathing report from certain public school officials referred to the film's "scatological content" — which, I discovered, has nothing to do with the songs of Ella Fitzgerald. No, the dictionary tells me, it has to do with "excrement or excremental functions."

The offence taken by these advisors was equally matched by the objections of feverish parents who left the film thinking of penicillin instead of parable.

"What if my kid sees this and tries it out?" was just one of the many horrified concerns from vulnerable mothers and fathers who felt their offspring were now in a position to do them in with a smile and a homemade pie.

The truth is, their children were meant to learn something much nobler than how to poison their family and playmates. *Pies* is an important film. Its lesson could not

be more relevant for our times, when intolerance so often rules the day. After all, the film ends on a truly uplifting note of redemption and reconciliation.

The case that I made to anyone who seemed to miss the point was that *Pies* is about bringing people together — and that we can't get to this place of healing unless we first start with the wounds we inflict on each other.

"Oh, really!" cried the multicultural group in Saskatchewan. "We'll see about that!" and they bristled all the way to the Prime Minister's office (or so I was told) demanding the film be banned from distribution. And apparently, the "scatological content" wasn't their main concern. It was the movie's depiction of Germans and Poles that riled them the most (although I'm sure the poo couldn't have helped).

The film didn't stand a chance. *Pies* received very little recognition except for a Blue Ribbon Award from one major film festival in New York (a city, I'm happy to say, that still honours alleged artistic depravity).

The main distributor for *Pies* was me, visiting schools and throwing light on the oft-forgotten commandment about loving thy neighbour. Kids overwhelmingly adored the movie. The more manure the better, and they took the film's message of forgiveness to heart. These screenings were wonderful sounding boards for discussing prejudice and how to turn it around.

At the time, I couldn't figure it out. Why was *Pies* being relegated to the back burner of the NFB's promotional campaign? Yes, the subject matter was controversial, but that could work in the film's favour. Surely the NFB marketers were discovering that children responded to the film with genuine enthusiasm, as I witnessed first-hand. More importantly, these students were learning an extremely valuable life lesson about getting along with others. Were the marketing experts, who have the power to stop a film in its tracks, not taking into account that their target audience — kids themselves — was overwhelmingly endorsing the film and benefiting from it?

My answer came later, much later. Fast forward twenty-five years . . .

I'm sitting at my computer. An email pops up, reproduced here exactly as I received it:

Hi, my name is Mark, and when I was about 8 (or so), my teacher & class at Tyndall Park Elementary School, in Winnipeg, was chosen (for whatever reason) to screen and review short films for the National Film Board of Canada. This was way back in 1983, or 1984, somewhere around there. So we did get to see *Pies*. We thought it was great! Everyone was laughing and applauding, except for our teacher. Usually at the end of each film, she would ask us some questions, and she'd fill out some papers with comments from her, and from the class. Even though the class loved it, our teacher was really disgusted by it, and when it was over, she didn't do the usual 'question period.' Later, when we were going out for recess, or lunch, or whatever it was, I saw the paper that she had to fill out, and send back to the NFB, it was full of lies. She said we didn't like it, it wasn't suitable for children, etc., etc. So, not that it matters too much, 25 years later, but the 'review' was a lie, we enjoyed your film, and I hope that her lies didn't affect funding or distribution of this or any other of your works.

—Mark P

Wow! By the last sentence my eyes stopped blinking and my mouth dropped open. What a message to get out of the blue! And how incredible to discover a teacher's deliberate misrepresentation so many years after the fact!

Here is my reply, expressed publicly for all to read, to an exemplary student, and the adult he became:

Dear Mark,

I am very moved by what you did then and what you have done now by writing me. It gives me faith that, one way or another, people don't really get away with misdeeds—not as long as individuals like you are around. In your own small way you are a Bearer of Truth, a real hero in my eyes!

As for your teacher from Tyndall Park Elementary School, possibly retired now with plenty of time to browse through bookshops, may she come across this very book (perhaps its author's name conjures up some distasteful memory that she can't quite put her finger on) and flip to this very page, and be shocked to discover how the exploits of a long-forgotten student demonstrated more decency and integrity than she could ever imagine.

And so, yes, Mark, it does matter, especially twenty-five years later. Thank you for setting the record straight. S.C.

1986–98 THE YEAR(S) OF THE CAT

THEY SAY THAT cats have nine lives. My next project, *Snow Cat*, based on a short story by the late Dayal Kaur Khalsa, had as many incarnations:

1. Starting as a ten-minute film with a Canada Council grant,
2. Becoming an NFB "half-hour" TV co-production for Teletoon,
3. Surviving a dissolved partnership between myself and another film company,
4. Re-grouping with a new outside executive producer,
5. Re-scripting with live actors integrated throughout the animation,
6. Re-scripting a second time with a live-action host and the rest of the film fully animated,
7. Re-scripting a third time with an animated grandmother for the intro and extro,
8. Re-scripting a fourth and final time with a beautiful screenplay by author Tim Wynne-Jones,
9. ... And, finally, re-cutting a fifteen-minute DVD version for a compilation release.

1998
from Jean-Michel Labrosse's
finger-paint animation
(please see the chapter on
'End Credits' for fuller details
of his extraordinary work on
the Snow Cat production)

SOMETIMES ARTISTS STRAY too far from home. I spent over ten years trekking up hills and down valleys seeking that elusive cat of snow and never truly finding it.

It was only recently, when I came across my very first storyboard for the Canada Council, now yellowed with age, when it struck me. My original idea was so simple and pure. It was perfect.

Had I not been driven by blockbuster ambitions that can easily blind a filmmaker, I would have seen that the *Snow Cat* I was looking for was on my doorstep all the while.

I must say that I don't regret the search. In the end, it was part of an artist's journey that brought me to some of the most remarkable moments of my career.

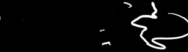

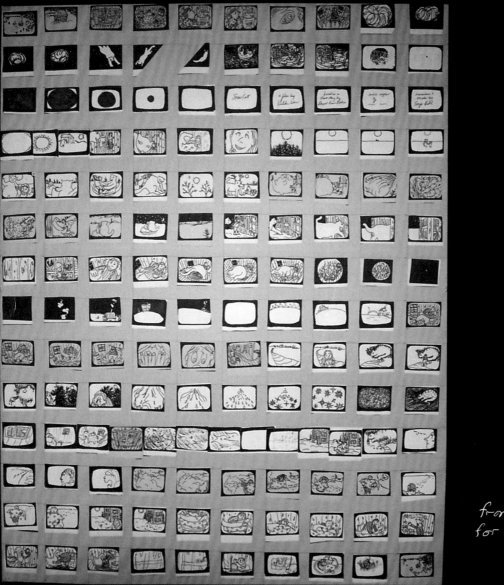

1986
from my original Snow Cat storyboard
for the Canada Council

ON A BLIND DATE WITH MAUREEN STAPLETON

"LEFT! LEFT!" HER booming voice is unmistakable. I recognize that raspy timbre from all the mega-hits she starred in: Warren Beatty's *Reds*; Woody Allen's *Interiors*; even the 1960s musical *Bye Bye Birdie*. Here is one of the greatest actresses of all time — a triple Oscar-, Emmy-, and Tony-winning Hollywood legend — screaming at me from the passenger seat of the rented car I'm driving.

"I said *left*!" she bellows again, using the full projection of her theatrical training.

Oh God, why do I always get that wrong? It's like I have some mild brain disorder that crosses my wires when it comes to left and right. Maybe it has something to do with being left-handed. Or maybe it's just because I'm totally spaced out finding myself in a car with Maureen Stapleton. But for whatever reason, I'm making the wrong turn at the intersection and have to veer dramatically (so to speak) in the opposite direction.

To be clear, it's just the two of us, Sheldon and Maureen, never having met before, travelling along a quaint honeymoon-like country road in the Berkshire Mountains. I know it's springtime, I remember that much. But is it cloudy or a bright blue sky? I don't recall — only that it is relatively warm, because Maureen Stapleton is wearing a housecoat.

Your first reaction must be, "Is he dreaming?" Even to me, it feels like some wild imagining. However, what I am describing actually happened, which must lead to your next question: "How in God's name did he end up in a rented car in the Berkshires with Maureen Stapleton?"

To fully answer this, I must go back many years.

It's 1986. I'm in an office that appears to be more from the 1950s, with dark wood paneling on the walls and bevelled glass on the door. I feel like I'm at the doctor's, expecting a receptionist in a powder blue cardigan and little starched nurse's cap to ask me if this is my first visit.

Instead, my publisher's assistant pokes her head in and says, "May's earlier meeting is going a bit longer than expected. She'll be out in a few minutes."

She's referring to May Cutler, the founder and president of Tundra Books. These were the days before McClelland and Stewart took the little Montreal company under its wing and relocated it to a much cushier nest in Toronto.

Within a short time, May emerges, followed by a woman dressed in white — all white: a white cotton robe over white baggy pants with white canvas sneakers which make sharp, squeaky noises against the varnished floor. But the most striking part of her outfit is a multi-folded turban wrapped high on top of her head and shaped like a giant white beehive.

May sees me in the corner. "Oh, hello, Sheldon." She turns back to the woman in white. "Dayal, come meet the illustrator of *The Hockey Sweater*."

I liked Dayal Kaur Khalsa from that first moment of our brief introduction. Over the next decade, I came to know more of the story behind this brilliant author/artist and her most fascinating journey: a Jewish girl formerly from Brooklyn who immigrated to Canada and joined an ashram as a devout "nun" (as she referred to herself), having converted to the Sikh faith and leaving behind a string of husbands along the way. How could I not like her?

Her humour was what attracted me the most. Those who met her couldn't wait to hear what she would say next. We became good friends in spite of our limited contact. The bond between us held fast as kindred spirits who shared a very similar approach to our art — except for one main difference. I relied on the writings of others; she illustrated her own stories.

Dayal passed away at the height of her career after battling cancer for a number of years, but not before completing a glorious body of work, even while undergoing intense radiation treatment.

"I'm so glad you're the one animating my stories and not me," she confided near the end of her struggle. "I couldn't deal with them."

I was already in production adapting her mythological tale, *Snow Cat*, to film. I felt that telling me this was her way of gratefully passing along her well-used paintbrush so that I could carry on her legacy through animation.

But "stories"? Why did she refer to "them," plural? I was only animating one. I let it pass. Must be the morphine talking.

As it turned out, it wasn't.

Soon after *Snow Cat* was released (sadly, Dayal did not live to see the final product), I unexpectedly began the animation of another Khalsa tale, *I Want a Dog*. It seemed to happen in a flash! The idea appeared, the storyboard flowed out of me, and the NFB program committee readily agreed to fund the project. I still remember producer Marcy Page's surprise at the ease with which the project was passed.

"Almost every submission was rejected or sent back for revision, but —" she happily announced, "— *I Want a Dog* sailed through."

Did Dayal know there would be more Khalsa projects in the cards for me when she said "stories"? But I'm getting ahead of myself. I only bring up *I Want a Dog* now to mention that little bit of fortune-telling by Dayal at the end of her life. In fact, she, herself, consulted with a psychic on occasion. His name was Fred. He resided in a southwestern community in United States, somewhere in the desert, carrying on a business of long-distance phone sessions.

I actually called Fred myself, soon after Dayal died, while I was working on *Snow Cat*. It was a shot in the dark, but I was hoping he could shed some light on Maureen Stapleton. I was sure that Dayal had mentioned the actress's name to me many years earlier, but no one I asked now knew what I was talking about. Dayal told me that some producers from Hollywood wanted to create a live-action version of her children's book, *Tales of a Gambling Grandma*, and that they wanted Maureen Stapleton to play the part of her grandmother. I remember how delighted Dayal was.

I never heard mention of it again. Dayal never spoke of the film or Maureen Stapleton after that, but it stuck with me for some reason. A seed was planted in my mind that Maureen Stapleton should be the one to tell the story of *Snow Cat* in my film.

Was this some crazy whim on my part, or did Dayal actually bring up the actress's name? I was hoping that Fred could connect with Dayal in the afterlife, and ask her on my behalf.

When I got through to Fred, I was a bit disconcerted to find out that he was actually an *animal* psychic. I had forgotten that Dayal used to seek his advice about her two cats. Perhaps my snow cat, even though animated, was enough to qualify, because Fred accepted my request to contact Dayal.

"Give me a moment," he said.

I sat with the phone to my ear, listening.

Dead silence.

I held the receiver closer, waiting for any communications.

More silence.

I felt the seconds tallying up on my long-distance phone bill.

Nothing. Were we disconnected?

Then Fred's voice:

"Sorry, she's not available now," he informed me matter-of-factly.

"Oh," I replied, not knowing what that meant. It was almost like he was her secretary telling me she was busy and to try again later. I didn't suppose I could leave a message, so I said goodbye and made my own decision about Maureen Stapleton.

Hence, here I am, on the way to a voice recording, chauffeuring the actress in my rented car.

We're weaving through the Berkshires, looking for the local sound studio where Miss Stapleton (I'm not sure how to address her at this point) will narrate the story of *Snow Cat*. I was surprised when her agent arranged that I be the one to transport his client from her little apartment outside of Lenox, Massachusetts.

As we drive, she isn't saying very much (except for vociferously pointing out my left from my right). I don't know what to talk about. I try to break the awkwardness.

"I thought you would be living in a big mansion in Hollywood."

As soon as I utter the words, I realize what a stupid thing I've said, but I am curious, though, that she lives in such ordinary surroundings. And she didn't change out of her housecoat. Since I picked her up, I haven't detected any more glamour from her than if I was meeting my aunt in the suburbs — except for that photo.

I saw it out of the corner of my eye when Maureen went to find her keys before we left her apartment. It was pinned to the fridge with kitchen magnets: an 8×10 glossy photo, slipping down to one side: Maureen Stapleton and Elizabeth Taylor, a flash of a moment — two Hollywood legends in the limelight, radiant, shoulder to shoulder on stage. Their friendship seemed genuine in spite of all the glitter.

We drive on in silence. My mind races to come up with something to say. What else?

"Have you done other voices for animated films?"

That's a better ice-breaker, but her answer is interrupted by a series of coughing fits. Each time she starts to answer, her words get caught up in phlegm. These outbursts continue all the way to the studio. Oh my God, there is no way that she can do this recording!

What have I done? I convinced the National Film Board of Canada that Maureen Stapleton must be the narrator for *Snow Cat,* despite an ample choice of very accomplished Canadian actresses who ought to be considered before going to the States. Plus a good chunk of the budget has now been eaten up because of this fool notion of mine. But I was so sure it was meant to be! If only Dayal hadn't been busy with other astral matters, she could have warned me.

These are my thoughts when we get to the studio. The sound engineer is checking the microphone level and Maureen is hacking away in a corner.

"Maybe I should look at the script," she finally says in between coughs. "It's about a cat?"

Oh my God, again! She hasn't even read the script! This is a nightmare! I can never face them back home. I'll just keep driving south and start fresh in Mexico.

The large speakers click on. The sound engineer is ready. "Miss Stapleton, let's begin with a read-through. Take 1, *Snow Cat.*"

Maureen's voice fills the room.

"*Try to imagine what it must have been like living just at the edge of the woods, far, far away in the North, all by yourself. The only face you ever see is your own. That's how Elsie lived.*"

Not one cough. Not one trace of hesitation. It's as if she wrote the story herself. She describes the Snow Cat's creation with the perfect tone of awe and mystery:

"*Ah, but this was no ordinary cat. His teeth and bones were made from icicles, and his eyes from hailstones, and as for the rest, he was made completely out of snow.*"

109

The actress's arms wave through the air like a conductor commanding a symphony, matching the cadence of each phrase with the rhythm of her movements.

"It was so calm and cozy in the little house, and they were so tired from their adventures, that before they knew it, both Elsie and Snow Cat fell fast asleep."

Maureen's delivery is effortless. I'm mesmerized. Everything becomes still in this little valley in the Berkshire Mountains as she tells the story of the Snow Cat.

"Soon it was time for the flock to leave. It's just how it is with wild things."

In what feels like no time, she reaches the end of the narration, never stopping once.

"... and a heart holds memories, and memories forever more hold the ones we love."

I turn away from the sound engineer. I don't want him to see that I'm crying. He'll probably think it's because the ending is so touching, but really it's because of Maureen Stapleton. Her gift. The tears are gratitude. I have never experienced such pure genius right before my eyes.

The second reading is unnecessary, but we record it anyway. It's a wrap, as they say.

I'm in love with Maureen. I look to the actress to see if she is as taken with her achievement as much as I am. What is it like for her, I wonder, to have delivered such a masterful narration?

Ah, she wants to tell me something.

"Psst. You got wheels, honey? Do me a favour?"

Maureen motions to me in between coughs. "Can you take me to the grocery store?"

An hour later, I pull into the parking lot of her apartment complex. She's happy to be home. I help her out with her shopping bag filled with tins of mandarin oranges and a bottle of sparkling rosé. Our conversation has become much friendlier, more relaxed.

She bows slightly. "You're a gentleman and a scholar."

I'm not so sure about the scholar part, but being a gentleman, I shake her hand and say thank you.

As I watch her cough her way down the courtyard path, my heart is full. I'm thinking, until the day I die, I will never forget the most magical performance by a woman in a housecoat.

1998
THE INTERVIEW

WHAT IF THE entire time I say *amination* instead of *animation*?

I'm teaching at Harvard University. I never applied, nor ever dreamed I'd be here. An unexpected phone call came in March to my Montreal house. I was offered a stint as Visiting Lecturer at the Carpenter Center, and now I'm in Cambridge the following September, about to meet students who want to enrol in my course.

Sitting alone, I wait for the first applicant to enter the century-old office assigned to me. This is what I'll say:

"Hello, are you applying for Film *Amination*? Please sit down. Tell my why you'd like to be an *aminator*."

They wouldn't have enough nerve to correct me. What could they say? But of course I'll never do it. I'm more nervous than they are.

A student shows up. I greet her.

"Hello, are you applying for Film Animation? Please sit down. Tell me why you'd like to be an animator."

The interviewing begins and I soon discover that none of the applicants will ever be animators. They are future doctors, chemical engineers, computer scientists, astrophysicists looking to fill up their credit requirements with an off-beat side course.

I begin to feel queasy. After two hours, the little room is spinning with so much intellect that my brain may soon explode. I've only interviewed six applicants and there are three times as many left on the list.

My questions repeat each time around: "Why do you want to learn Animation? What kind of film do you want to make?"

And then the seventh student: "I want to do something with playdough."

Finally! Yes! Someone I can relate to! My head clears! I love playdough — the colours, the texture. Every time I smell it, I want to eat it.

I lean forward, invigorated. "Tell me more. What exactly would you do?"

"I was thinking of adapting his *Allegory of the Cave.*"

"Excuse me?"

"You know, his story from *The Republic*. Am I the first one to suggest something with Plato? Sir, are you okay?"

A PLATONIC POST-SCRIPT to the Harvard Class of '98–'99 . . .

Dear students,

It is with great fondness that I remember each one of you and your projects. Every so often I come across the show-reel from that year. There isn't an 'Allegory of the Cave' in the mix. (After a few Dialogues we drew the logical conclusion that a film with Plato is not nearly as easy as making one with playdough.) But watching all your different little movies roll by, I'm touched by the enriching experience of our brief time together.

When it came to Academia, you were a school of fish and I was a fish out of water, but we met on a level playing field, not unlike a kindergarten playground. I was able to get you to tap into something fresh and passionate in your creations. By doing this, I know I succeeded as an instructor, but you also demonstrated something to me.

Many of you were preparing for careers in front of microscopes and test tubes and nuclear reactors.

Your schedules could have crushed the most conscientious of students. And yet, there you were, week after week, working on your projects with so much heartfelt enthusiasm and carefree delight. I felt the innocent joy that floated through your animated visions!

In spite of the demanding course load you faced, under all the pressures and responsibilities, I saw the playful kid in you, always only a scratch away. You proved what many great artists expounded through the ages: Something young must stay alive in us in order to create. In fact, you guys were way ahead of Picasso. He confessed it took him a lifetime to paint like a child.

Thank you for that inspiring year!

Sincerely yours,

Professor Cohen

Film Amination, Harvard University

A newspaper clipping from *The Harvard Crimson* of me with a student's work.

2003
THE YEAR OF THE DOG

SOMETIMES A PROJECT is pure joy from beginning to end. It just unfolds naturally and the director's main task is simply not to interfere with the flow.

Such was the case with *I Want a Dog* (as mentioned before, written by *Snow Cat* author Dayal Kaur Khalsa). From the very first square of my storyboard, I could feel the doo-wop tempo begin to pulsate and it never let up until the last frame of animation.

BY THE WAY, you know that perplexing question that so many of us from the 1950s and '60s have pondered:

"Who put the bop in the bop shoo bop shoo bop?"

I finally know the answer: It's Zander Ary and Neko Case. (Check out the *I Want a Dog* credits at the end of this book!)

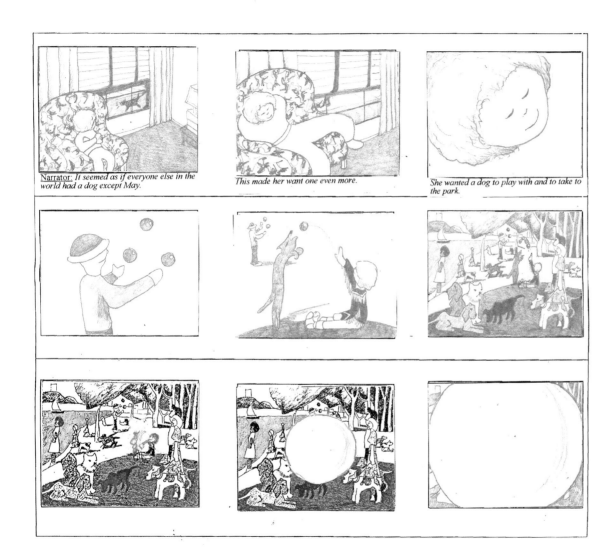

Narrator: *It seemed as if everyone else in the world had a dog except May.*

This made her want one even more.

She wanted a dog to play with and to take to the park.

A page from the *I Want a Dog* storyboard

2006
THE ROAD TO
ABU DHABI

"WHERE? ARE YOU crazy!" These were the first words my wife said to me when I told her I had been invited to show my films in the United Arab Emirates.

"Don't worry," I said. "It's totally safe. I already checked on Google. Abu Dhabi's a big hotspot for tourists."

"Isn't that where Garfield always sent Nermal?" my twenty-two-year-old son piped in. I smiled, recalling one of our favourite cartoon TV shows from his childhood days. A Saturday morning ritual, we would start the weekend together watching that big, devious orange cat stuff his much cuter purple nemesis into a box and mail him to what sounded like a make-believe destination.

But, indeed, Abu Dhabi is a real place. If you look on a map, to the right of Saudi Arabia and left of Oman, you'll discover this desert principality — one of seven, including Dubai, that are part of a federation of states called the United Arab Emirates.

Fifty years ago, in Montreal, while Ray Stevens wailed through the plastic speakers of my 1960s transistor radio singing his number one hit about Ahab and his camel

Clyde, the inhabitants of Abu Dhabi were living in mud-made dwellings halfway across the world. They followed traditions from thousands of years ago, spending their days in search of pearls in the blue-green Gulf to the north.

Almost overnight, the tiny cultured treasures they collected were replaced with an unexpected giant crude one — a massive reserve of thick, black oil that quickly propelled Abu Dhabi and nearby Dubai into a glistening oasis of Manhattan-like skyscrapers and Western-style shopping malls. It seemed to appear in the blink of an eye, the birth of modern times, heralded by the country's beloved leader, Sheikh Zayed bin Sultan Al Nahyan. His vision was far-reaching and was shared by subsequent members of the al Nahyan family who continued to open up the UAE to people from cultures and countries in every part of the world . . . including a few of us Canadians.

The invitation read:

Under the patronage of His Excellency Sheikh Nahyan bin Mubarak al Nahyan, the Embassy of Canada is hosting a week of cultural and educational exchange and celebration on reading and literacy. This week-long program is designed to increase awareness of the richness of Canadian children's culture through opportunities to meet critically acclaimed and multi-award-winning Canadian authors, illustrators, and performers.

NOT KNOWING WHAT to expect, our critically acclaimed group began to gather at Toronto's Pearson Airport, all of us slightly bewildered, like first-time campers about to be swept off in a big orange school bus out of the city for the summer. But this was winter, a frosty February morning, and we were about to board an Etihad Airways jumbo jetliner — travelling Pearl Business Class — for the distant city of Abu Dhabi, to return after ten sun-soaked days of intercultural exchange.

We met at the ticket counter — a diverse, creative contingent representing Canada, each of us an entertainer of children in our own particular way: through song

(Winnipeg's Fred Penner and his accompanist, Paul O'Neil); through words (Ottawa's Rachna Gilmore, Vancouver's Paul Yee, Toronto's Paulette Bourgeois, Maxine Trottier from Newman's Cove, and, of course, Montreal's Roch Carrier along with his wife, Nina). Finally, I came into the picture, through film and drawing, along with Port Hope's Brenda Clarke, who illustrated Paulette's ever popular *Franklin the Turtle* stories.

"Flight EY205 to Abu Dhabi, please proceed to the boarding gate."

Before leaving behind our home and native land, we posed for a parting photo, all of us excited to set off for a foreign destination we had only read about or seen in pictures.

I bade a silent farewell to the big, furry RCMP moose behind us — this adorable mascot for our national security — and then began to wonder, "What world were we really about to enter?"

My thoughts were turning darker. Each step closer to the awaiting plane brought another imaginary news flash from the Middle East. After years of watching eleven o'clock reports, the scenes were all embroiled into an

From left to right: Roch Carrier; his wife, Nina; me; Brenda Clarke; and Paul Yee

apocalyptic montage: demonstrators chanting, riotous mobs burning effigies, war zones erupting in chaos. Could my wife's fears be right?

Hold on. We were going to the United Arab Emirates, after all. I quickly refreshed my thoughts with those lush Google images of velvet green golf courses rising out of the endless sand dunes; an indoor ski resort sheltered from the brutal desert sun, fully equipped with artificial snow packed onto an artificial mountain; and translucent turquoise water cradling man-made islands that, when seen from the sky, fan out like the leaves of a perfectly symmetrical palm tree. It was time to relax.

As the plane sailed eastward, high above the frozen farmlands of Canada, I could sit back and enjoy the tiny smoked salmon canapés being served by the exotic stewardess. "Would you like some champagne to go with your meal?" she graciously offered from behind semi-veiled headwear. My adventure had begun!

"AVOID EATING WITH your left hand. Never show the soles of your feet." Highly sensitive issues about what is regarded as dirty and offensive in this part of the world. I studied the official etiquette provided by the Canadian Embassy as I sat in the room assigned to me at the Sands Hotel in the heart of Abu Dhabi. The last thing I wanted to do was to insult anyone here on our first evening in the city where each of us was settling into our respective rooms that would become our home base for the next week.

It could have been any hotel room you would find in North America with the same generic décor: tasteful curtains and bedspread, high-end picture frames on the wall, a phone on the nightstand with a direct line to the front desk, a TV with remote, and a sparkling clean bathroom with that sweet, soapy smell which greets every traveller back home.

But when you pulled back the curtains, you knew this was a very different world. It was sunset. Most of my view was obstructed by two sand-coloured concrete apartment buildings filling the entire block. They housed what appeared to be immigrant workers whose laundry hung from hundreds of railings and windows in the many jam-packed quarters, top to bottom.

In the small space between buildings I could see a thin orange line of fading daylight tracing the desert horizon. Then I heard it: the plaintive cries of evening prayers rising up from every corner of the city. It was impossible not to feel something stir—a mournful, ancient memory. It was beautiful and it was frightening, alone in my hotel room, so far from everything that was familiar.

TIME TO JOIN the others. In a few minutes, everyone would be regrouping in the hotel lobby to be chauffeured to the opening night VIP cocktail reception. Our event, entitled "Celebrate Canada," was being launched at the lavish Cultural Foundation where His Excellency the Minister of Education would be extending an official welcome by cutting the ribbon of a Canadian Photography and Art Exhibit.

It was an impressive building. I was especially struck by the series of camel sculptures outside the windows lining the entrance. Each camel was hand-painted in unique designs by selected artists from different regions of the UAE.

I later imagined (in Photoshop) what my own contribution might have been had I been asked:

But now, waiting for the Sheikh to arrive, my musings weren't quite as playful. Dressed up in my almost never-worn black suit (I could now add ribbon-cuttings to weddings and funerals), I began to review the formalities that the Canadian Embassy briefed us on. I wasn't worried about showing the soles of my feet, but not eating with my left hand — that same left hand that animated films and illustrated books — the one that brought me to this prestigious event in the first place . . . I had my doubts! If I wasn't careful, I was only one dip away from causing an international incident with the VIP hors d'oeuvres.

And so, cocktail in hand (my right hand), I mingled (without a plate) through the crowd of tray-carrying hostesses and mouth-stuffing guests. I would have to find a way to celebrate Canada that didn't involve too much eating.

Our little group buzzed with excitement.

"Did you know only fifteen percent of the population in the UAE are true Emirati?"

"What are Emirati?"

"The men you see in the white robes and those head-dresses. They're part of the original families from way back."

"What about the women?"

"Make sure you don't take their pictures. It's considered very rude here."

"Wouldn't it be rude if you did that anywhere?"

"I heard the women wear really fancy clothes underneath their robes, but they have to cover up when they go out."

"I don't get it, why would you go through the trouble of getting all dressed up and then just hide yourself in black?"

"I think they're only supposed to look pretty for their husbands."

"Someone told me if an Emirati marries another Emirati, they get a free mansion to live in."

"And all I got was a lousy duplex."

"I guess that makes you —"

The room went silent. What happened?

I heard someone whisper, "Oh, look! The Sheikh!"

With quiet, majestic strides, he strutted through the crowd who obediently fell to either side of his entourage. Like Charlton Heston (if not Moses himself) he parted the sea of people, holding a pair of golden scissors (if not a wooden staff), ready to cut the silky red ribbon at the entrance to the exhibit.

I have never experienced that sense of awe and reserve for our own Canadian leaders. We've all seen those well-aimed cream pies being flung at the smiling faces of unsuspecting Ottawa politicians. I could only imagine what the punishment in the UAE would be for assault and battery with whipped cream.

THE WEEK PROCEEDED in a whirlwind mix of book readings, film screenings, and concert singing, each presenter adhering to an individual schedule with elementary school kids, university students, and general family audiences.

For my presentation in particular, I wondered how everyone would respond when I showed them a film about something so foreign to their daily lives. Would they be able to relate to *The Sweater*'s story about life in snowy Quebec?

I asked the students, "How many of you feel that your parents sometimes don't understand you and make you do things that you really don't want to do?"

Immediately hands would wave in the air, heads would bob up and down. Little Roch's plight of having to wear the dreaded blue sweater amongst all the red number 9s hit home in the same way it does with kids in Canada. Snow or sand—it made no difference. It was universal. They easily empathized with the young protagonist facing this childhood calamity.

BECAUSE MY LECTURE included movies, I was assigned my own personal projectionist, whose name was Shariff. I came to think of him as The Wizard of Oz, invisible to the audience, but orchestrating every slide and film onto the giant movie screen from his little hidden booth in the back of the theatre.

I began to notice, however, that Shariff would quietly appear in the audience out of nowhere, always at the same time. It was when *I Want a Dog* played. I discovered that he loved the movie and he loved the music and he wanted to experience it up close. I know why. There is something about the addictive doo-wop soundtrack and especially the allure of Neko Case's sultry vocals that Shariff couldn't resist. Even in an admittedly fluffy children's animated short, Neko Case has the power to melt any listener's heart with a certain purity and longing in her voice. Not unlike the prayers from mosques, her singing seems to rise out of the soul.

No, I wasn't surprised to see Shariff swooning to "*. . . I want a puppy, one who will love me, I want a puppy of my ve-ry, ve-ry own-n-n-n.*"

OUR HOSTS AT the Embassy made certain that business was generously mixed with pleasure. Revered lecturers one minute, we became googly-eyed tourists the next: palace hopping, market buying, and camel riding.

I often felt like we were characters in an Agatha Christie novel, an eclectic group of artists, writers, and performers thrown together in exotic circumstances. It seemed like it was only a matter of time before one of us would fail to show up at the large, round dining room table in the hotel restaurant where we met every night for the sumptuous complimentary buffet. I could see one of the chapters beginning something like this:

Sheldon of Arabia

"Oh, my darlings, this fish is heaven," Rachna said in between bites. "By the way, has anyone seen Paul Yee? He's been missing since breakfast."

But, of course, no one disappeared, although I wouldn't have been surprised to find out that Fred Penner had been carted off by the authorities. At a command performance for the Sheikh's daughter, Fred (who obviously never read the etiquette rules) couldn't control his "Dancing Heels." There he was on stage, brazenly flouting the soles of his shoes as he sang with wild abandon about his "hap, hap, happy feet."

IT APPEARS THAT crime in the UAE has a much lower incidence rate than in Western cities. A tour guide told us, "Don't worry about anything getting stolen. Even if you leave your laptop on a park bench, no one would dare take it because they'd be afraid of the consequences."

Whether true or not, we all felt perfectly safe wherever we went. Well, actually, let me correct that. I did experience one night of mild terror. It happened the evening before our flight home.

We're on a final farewell trip at a Bedouin outpost in the desert, being treated to a meal under the stars. It's all pleasant conversation over traditional dishes that, if we were true nomads, would be eaten, as the custom goes, with only three fingers.

Someone shrieks! It's coming from the far end of the dining area.

A belly dancer, having emerged unseen from a hidden tent, begins to drag helpless onlookers onto a makeshift stage. She forces them to perform humiliating gyrations, each one more grotesque than the next. She stops at no one: men, women — it makes no difference. Stunned Westerners are being herded on stage against their wills, smiling sheepishly as their middle-aged hips try desperately to catch up with the relentless pounding of a Middle Eastern drumbeat.

Now she's coming towards our table, seeking one more cowering victim to whirl into her wily dervish. Cornered by crossed-legged colleagues on either side of me, I freeze and quietly pray by everything holy under the desert stars, "Please don't pick me. Please don't pick me."

No use. She's fast approaching, silver bracelets jangling up and down her arms, beaded tassels rippling from her curves. I'm in her crosshairs; she targets me with a fixed smile. I try to look busy. I pick up my plate. I eat my cous-cous. One mouthful. Another mouthful. I even use three fingers.

She stops dead, her smile gone.

What?

Her face contorts into a look of revulsion.

I don't understand.

She's staring at the food in my *left* hand.

I'm saved!

OTHER THAN THAT, it was a perfectly calm and enjoyable adventure in a part of the world few of us in the West know much about.

And that's the point, isn't it? We are all so afraid of that which is unfamiliar. And we make judgements about those who are seemingly not like us.

But are we really that different? So what if, at the end of another Fred Penner concert, one little girl asked him why they didn't just kill the cat that kept coming back? Is that not similar to my son watching that other pesky cat, Garfield, seal a box stuffed with a cute little innocent, and admittedly annoying, kitty inside named Nermal and mail him to the far reaches of Abu Dhabi? Are children not children all over the world? East, West — is it not time that the twain shall meet?

As I flew back home, my thoughts rested on the massive sand dunes I had sat atop just the day before in the fading sunlight at the end of our journey.

Out the jetliner window, far down below, snow-clad mountain peaks of other foreign lands were already replacing the desert. The steady hum of the plane buoyed my contemplative mood.

As I turned away from the window, my eye was drawn to a brochure tucked in the netted compartment in front of me. Like the message you find in a fortune cookie, the motto on the Etihad Airline pamphlet seemed directed at me. *"Change the way you see the world."*

And I did. I was returning enriched, my heart full of the warmth of my travels. We're not that different after all. And where we are different, then let's be fascinated and allow others to be different. Let's not only allow it, but let's celebrate it. Celebrate Canada. Celebrate the United Arab Emirates. Why not celebrate every country, every culture, and every religion on this vast, spinning globe that we all share?

The sparkles of pink champagne were bubbling into my brain, everything merging and mixing: prayers of the soul; towers rising from mosques; doo-wop music and *I Want a Dog*. The plane floated through an endless stream of amorphous clouds as I drifted off . . . people applauding . . . Ed Sullivan in a chequered headdress . . . "Ladies and gentlemen, let's hear it for Neko Case and the Minarettes!"

I WOKE UP on the other side of the ocean, a splattering of tiny lights on the ground below, windows of huddled communities shimmering in the dark. This didn't have to be such a hateful world. Why fear those not like us? Why not embrace each other's existence? Why not respect one another's place with a sense of the humanity in us all?

"Excuse me." The stewardess' voice broke into my reverie. "We'll be landing shortly. Seat-back up, please."

She removed the empty champagne glass from my tray and replaced it with a fresh copy of a popular international newspaper, the headlines bold and stark:

BLAST WIDENS MIDEAST RIFT: 15 KILLED

2010
NO ANGLO
LEFT BEHIND

I CAN'T BELIEVE I won't reach enlightenment because of my gurgling stomach. How come no one else's stomach in the group makes noises? Maybe it's my Jewish genes modified over five centuries by consuming onions fried in chicken fat. If I was in a synagogue, I'd never worry like this. My stomach would just naturally blend in with all the other worshippers.

But I've taken it upon myself to meditate, and where better to practise the art of relaxation and calm inner being than in a traditional Buddhist centre, right? Unfortunately, not for me. By the end of a forty-five-minute sitting session, I usually become so tense in the utter stillness of the meditation hall that I can barely breathe, trying to squeeze off the high-pitched squeaks emanating from my belly. *"Stop! For God's sake, stop!"* That's what I'm screaming in my head as I clench my way to inner peace.

Today, however, I'm at ease attending a lecture by the resident lama who is removing the threatening silence with his comforting words on the importance of silently accepting things that threaten us. I believe this could qualify as my own personal *koan* (a little in-joke for Zen practitioners, which, yes, I'm clearly not).

Nevertheless, I'm among twenty or so other seekers, assembled together in half-lotus positions on the highly polished monastery floor. Cushioning each of our bottoms is a forest green round pillow on top of a thickly padded square mat. We're all intently jotting down essential answers to eternal questions as the young lama in a burgundy robe and golden yellow T-shirt finds the right English words to express the traditional Tibetan text of his native language. He is doing an excellent job of talking slowly and clearly so that we can all understand the wisdom filtering through him.

Except, at the end of each small part of his delivery, when he pauses briefly for us to take notes, a lady sitting near me continues to translate into French (in irritating whispers) what he has just said. She repeats one slow sentence after another, for her friend who does not understand English. I try to ignore it, but as the lecture goes on, it causes a significant delay that begins to disturb what started out as a vibrant, harmonious rhythm to the lama's presentation.

It doesn't seem right that twenty or thirty of us should have to wait for one person to catch up. I look to the lama for signs of his annoyance. Yet he just sits calmly, waiting for the lady to finish translating for her friend, after which he picks up the pace, as fresh and enthusiastic as before.

Why isn't he put off by these interruptions? He must feel it breaking the flow of his presentation even more than we do — and all for the sake of just one individual out of so many?

Then it clicks! Of course! This same situation which infuriates me, he welcomes whole-heartedly. This francophone woman who will otherwise miss the wisdom he wants to impart, is now able to receive it. He is actually encouraging the translation. He appreciates the deep commitment that these two friends have to this special kind of learning.

I close my notepad. My education is right here. It is an illuminating moment. I see that the sacred realm leaves no one behind. It needs each one of us as much as we need it. Staying whole is what really matters!

I remind myself of this essential truth whenever I feel out of place or ill at ease with others as I sometimes do. Roch Carrier, in his infinite wisdom, understood this truth when, those many years ago, he invited an unlikely team player such as myself to don his hockey sweater made of *pure laine*.

Illustrating
THE HOCKEY SWEATER

THANK YOU, MAY CUTLER

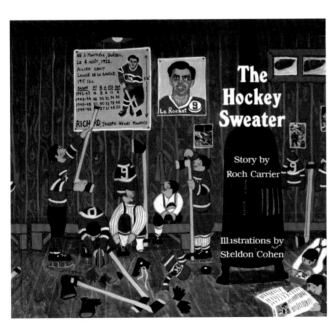

USUALLY THE BOOK comes first and then the movie, but in this case it was the opposite. It happened quite unexpectedly. It was 1982. I found myself with unfamiliar free time on my hands now that the *Sweater* movie was completed. I was enjoying a daily routine of long walks in my neighbourhood, contemplating what new possibilities might be waiting in the wings.

One afternoon I strolled by a bookstore and noticed a beautiful display of picture books in the window. It suddenly struck me!

"Why don't I do that with *The Sweater*!"

A children's book seemed like the perfect offshoot from the film. One particular cover caught my eye. The style of art was similar to mine and, by chance, the publisher was situated in Montreal.

Back at home, I searched through the phone book and then nervously dialled the number. Here is how I remember the events that followed.

The phone is ringing on the other end. My heart is racing. Someone picks up.

"Tundra Books."

"Hello, my name is Sheldon Cohen. I recently animated a movie called *The Sweater* for the National Film Board of Canada. It's based on a short story by author Roch Carrier. Would I be able to speak to someone about making it into a children's book?"

"One moment please."

I can hear the person who answered repeating my request to someone in the background. Within seconds the phone receiver comes to life with an excited voice on the other end.

"Hello, yes, this is May Cutler. My dear, do you know I've been wanting to do that story as a picture book since the day I heard it! When can you come in?"

And before I knew it, I was busy collaborating with Roch Carrier once again. To the author's delight, his boyhood exploits that had just found their way to the big screen would now also be relived inside the covers of children's book.

This project was no different than many I had undertaken. I was signing up for a job I knew nothing about. It was May Cutler who guided me from the start, switching my animator's hat to that of illustrator. At our first meeting, she told me to go buy some acrylics, get a bunch of masonite boards from the hardware store, and have them cut to size. Finally, when she saw me just standing there, she pointed to the door: "Now go home and paint!"

Her motto was "Children's Books as Art" and to her credit, the little company she founded was instrumental in giving Canadian picture books their world-class reputation for artistic excellence.

It was also May Cutler who decided to name the children's book what for many of you has become the household terminology for Roch's story, whether referring to book or film: *The Hockey Sweater*.

You probably think it would have been a cinch for me to go from movie to picture book. I thought so as well. After all, I had all my characters and settings completely worked out.

To my surprise, it took a full year to finish the paintings for the children's book. I learned that there are no shortcuts in any creative endeavour. The work itself sets its own parameters as to the amount of time and effort necessary to carry it out. I needed to respect the illustrations on their own terms (only thirteen in total) and approach them as a different entity than the animated cels (as you may recall, over ten thousand in total), even though both art forms were telling the exact same story.

1984 Salon du Livre, Montreal. Top row: Me (far left), Sorry, not sure who this is (centre), translator Sheila Fischman (far right). Bottom row: May Cutler (far left), Maurice Richard (center), Roch Carrier (far right).

ANIMATION VS. ILLUSTRATION

AS I GAINED more experience, I discovered that the determinant factor in the way that I deal with my job as animator on the one hand, and illustrator on the other, has to do with, actually . . . you.

Being a film director, I see my task as leading you through the story from one point to another. I must keep you on course without any distractions. Because I know your eyes can only focus on one object at a time, I try my hardest to keep your line of vision undisturbed.

In illustrating a picture book, however, the dynamics are the opposite. I encourage your eyes to wander. It is for that reason I love to add as many details as I can to my illustrations.

From the original mockup of *The Hockey Sweater*.

The beauty of an illustrated book is that you can physically hold it in your hands, turn the pages at your own pace, and actively find your way through the story—unlike the passive nature of watching a movie.

On the other hand, one can say that an animated film offers a reality that a picture book can't. It allows the story to jump off the page with characters who seem to have individual wills of their own.

IT IS WORTH pointing out that regardless of these differences between animation and illustration, I abide by the same guiding principles when I approach both art forms: for example, the need to let go of something that doesn't fit into the overall layout, no matter how much I want it to be there.

If you recall, this was my dilemma about including the Church statue in the artwork of one of the final animation backgrounds. I was convinced that it *should* be part of the design but could not position it properly, despite all the logic that told me to keep trying.

The exact same problem cropped up again when I was sketching the artwork for the picture book. It made complete sense to add the very same statue in question for the very same reason as before: it was the perfect symbol of authority for Roch's eviction from the game. I even threw in a cow this time, watching from the sidelines—a nosy witness to his humiliating trek through the snow.

For the picture book as for the animated film, my goal remained the same: to allow you to get inside Roch's skin and feel his emotional burden. But, once again, I had to accept that the most effective way for me to achieve this seemed to be by keeping the illustration starkly focused on the solitary figure—without the statue there (and, in this case, without the cow as well, which I especially found hard to resist).

I would like to share one further example where I learned to treat books and films as different entities, but with the same creative attitude towards both.

Here is the original rough drawing inserted into my mock-up for *The Hockey Sweater.*

An illustrator's "mock-up" is the equivalent of an animator's storyboard, serving as a blueprint for the whole project. Mock-ups are also referred to as "dummies," a term more appropriate, perhaps, to describe what illustrators often feel like going through the inevitable trials and errors that come up.

My intention for this particular drawing was to illustrate in the picture book what I had animated in the film: a swarm of moths devouring the Toronto sweater and a fantasy "bubble" of Rocket Richard shaking hands with the young boy.

But the more I looked at the mock-up, the more something kept bothering me about the illustration. (This is the benefit of having a mock-up as a dry run for the book.) The drawing wasn't working. Young Roch himself was getting lost in all the activity around him.

I decided to drop everything except the boy in prayer, with one little moth fluttering above him. As a result, the ending in the picture book has a different energy than in the movie — more understated.

The author originally told me to use his words as a springboard. I did so equally for both projects, and to my surprise, landed in different places. *The Sweater* movie finishes on a rousing note; *The Hockey Sweater* book, with a quieter resolution — in a way, an ending that is more in keeping with the atmosphere of the Church as I remember it.

The moths eating the jersey and the Rocket bubble were the two main components most obvious to include in my final illustration — and yet, you may note, they are nowhere to be found. Even now, if you were to say to me, "Shouldn't the Rocket be there?" I'd say, "Yes, a hundred percent. But it doesn't work. I don't know why."

PEOPLE HAVE SOMETIMES asked me which art form is my favourite: animation or illustration. I have considered the question this way:

The origin of the word animate is "to give spirit to" and the origin of the word illustrate is to "give light to."

And so which do I prefer?

I'm left without an answer. How can you choose between spirit and light?

A SERIES FOR ALL SEASONS

WITH *THE HOCKEY SWEATER* hot off the press, publisher May Cutler kept the laser drum rolling. She asked Roch Carrier to write three more short stories about his childhood featuring a different sport for each of the seasons. And so I found myself illustrating sequels for the next twelve years, off and on.

Which sport do you think the author chose for his spring story? I never would have guessed.

When the snow melts, the young hockey player reluctantly hangs up his ice skates for a pair of boxing gloves!

In *The Boxing Champion* (1991), Roch tells how he tried desperately to proclaim victory once and for all in the ritual boxing matches held every spring in the sprawling, open kitchen of his neighbours, the Côté family.

Because this was a story set with the season in full bloom, I was inspired to paint a springtime scene in all its glory. In nature, though, it is not always clear what one sees and does not see. I consciously played with this notion; some of the creatures are more camouflaged than others, but if you look carefully you can spot the following animals hidden in the artwork on the opposite page:

an owl
two chipmunks
a grasshopper
a praying mantis
a robin
a cat
a spider
a group of caterpillars
a ladybug
a bumblebee
a larva
a butterfly
Hint: Do you see the robin in the lilac tree?

At the time, I inserted this "hide-and-seek" aspect into the illustration so that my young son could play a game of finding all the animals. I must confess that if we were to play the game today, I would be the one searching and my son the one pointing them out.

EARLIER I WROTE about the connection between magic and art. The illustration above serves as an example of how an artist's canvas can hold something truly unexpected and mysterious.

It has to do with the dog included in the upper corner of the painting. Do you see it? (It's easier than finding the robin.)

I originally intended that to be our dog, K.C., who showed up twice before in the *The Hockey Sweater* illustrations.

And now I wanted to include him here in this new book. I set about painting his beige and white furry body sneaking freshly baked cookies from the little kitchen table. However, it never panned out. I tried many different versions but could not settle on the right image.

At some point I threw in the towel and painted any old dog that came to mind, which turned out to be a squat-shaped mutt with reddish-brown fur. It wasn't K.C., but so be it. This dog would do just fine.

A few days later, my wife went out for a walk with K.C. and returned shortly thereafter with a wandering stray that followed her back to our house. Aside from the fact that she left with one dog and came back with two, I could

hardly believe my eyes! Prancing through our front door was the very dog that I had painted in my illustration!

Once inside, this wayward pup flopped herself onto our dining room floor as if to say, "I'm here. Show me the love."

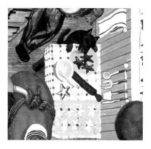

I knelt down and tickled her belly, in total amazement that this dog-out-of-nowhere had materialized as if from my painting.

"What should we call her?"

"Do you think K.C. will be jealous?"

"Does she have her shots?"

My wife and son and I bandied about these questions, when it occurred to me:

"Wait, maybe we're stealing someone's pet?"

A week later, we drove to the S.P.C.A. where we had left our metaphysical dog sheltered safely for public display, just in case there was a real owner out there looking for her.

"No one's claimed her," the volunteer told us. "She's all yours if you want her."

And so this hungry, abandoned creature became our wonderful, faithful "Cali" for the next fifteen years. What can I say, other than be careful what you draw because you never know what may show up outside your door! (Lucky for me there were no elephants in Sainte-Justine.)

ANOTHER POINT I'D like to make: The most effective art happens when it is close to home, from a place that touches the artist in some way. Whether making films or books, I rely on a heartfelt connection to guide me through the process.

When I was designing the layout of the same kitchen illustration, for instance, I began to fill it in with members of Roch's neighbours, the Côte family. It prompted a very fond memory of my own grandfather, who often sat off to one side whenever we had family gatherings. He'd be humming the "Song of the Volga Boatmen" and losing himself in his favourite hobby — making jigsaw puzzles — while my cousins and I ran around the house.

With that memory in mind, I decided to slip an elderly man into the illustration, quietly piecing together a puzzle in the corner of this boisterous scene.

He could very well have been my own grandfather, except in this case he would be humming a French-Canadian folksong instead of a Russian river ballad. Drawing on these common human roots, I was able to naturally find my way into Roch's childhood and make an authentic, meaningful connection to a place that would, otherwise, remain worlds apart.

SUMMER WAS NEXT. In *The Longest Home Run* (1994), Roch describes how baseball fever spread through his village after an incident involving two mysterious visitors from a travelling side-show.

"Step right up, come one, come all, see the greatest magician in the world . . . bringing secrets that will turn the world's philosophy upside down."

With these words the author announces the arrival of The Great Ratabaga and his daughter, Princess Adeline.

Roch told me that, as a young boy, he loved impressing his friends with magic tricks (and I would add that as an adult he continues to do so, only to a much larger audience, and using his stories as props).

In this tale of mischief, we meet the ever-cranky Sergeant Bouton, who is willing to overlook the antics of young Roch thinking he hit a baseball farther than any of the boys in the village.

Based on my talks in schools, I found that the illustration kids responded to the most was the one here, when the old man discovers it was not Roch, but a *girl* who surpassed all the boys! *"This is the end of the world!"* he cries out in horror. (Nothing like bulging eyes and wild nose-hairs to grab a child's attention.)

THE LAST OF the sequels is a story set in autumn. It introduces a sport that Roch knew nothing about.

In *The Basketball Player* (1996), Roch finds himself on his own for the first time at boarding school. Away from the comforts of home, the author-to-be is determined to find his way in the world. He's uncertain exactly what lies ahead, but he's excited to follow the path that is waiting for him.

When students are considering what they want to be when they grow up, I tell them, "Just choose something you love to do. And the best part of doing that is that others will love it, too."

This is the same message behind Roch Carrier's basketball story. He may not be suited for this sport, but he finds his true calling by sticking to his passion for reading and, eventually, for writing.

In the end, I'm happy to say that all is not lost on the basketball court either. Young Roch triumphantly makes the winning basket after struggling to measure up to the rest of the team.

In the final text of *The Basketball Player*, the author writes:

"In the photograph of the champions that autumn, I'm the one in the Montreal Canadiens sweater. I don't look like a champion. I am holding a book. I had started to read a great many books because I wanted to go far along the road of life."

Young Roch leaves home at the end of the series, confidently taking up a new mission as he enters the world on his own — in his words, "trying to become the Rocket Richard of the writers."

Keeping his childhood memories close to his heart, he carries with him the stories of his village, especially one about his beloved worn-out number 9 hockey sweater.

FLYING HIGH

IT ALMOST DIDN'T happen, but there was one more collaboration between Roch Carrier and myself after *The Hockey Sweater* series. I originally turned it down.

In 2003, the publisher requested that I illustrate the author's retelling of the Québécois legend *The Flying Canoe*. I simply had no clue how to approach the subject matter: French-Canadian voyageurs. Their treacherous canoe journeys to the interior Outaouais logging camps took place centuries ago. To me, they remained vague historical figures I studied in sixth grade.

When I spoke to Roch, he said that he had the very same reaction and hesitated in accepting this project.

"You mean you felt you couldn't do it either?" I was shocked.

He explained that he had strong doubts about taking it on, but once he gave it a chance, he found the right thread to tell his tale. If even Roch Carrier questioned himself, I felt the least I could do was to accept my own reservations and climb aboard with him.

After an awkward start, I soon found my way into the story and I'm happy to say that it was smooth sailing from then on. I've come to realize that, in the end, all art requires a leap of faith.

157

Evolution of an illustration from THE FLYING CANOE

"Don't be afraid. Forget perfection." This is what I tell myself when I have a big blank sheet of paper waiting to be filled in. The first step is to let it out, whatever bits and pieces come to mind.

It is barely discernible, but in that initial mess of lines and notes and half-shapes, the final painting is already there.

Art for me has always been about cleaning up that very first scribble.

ARTIST'S GALLERY

PAINTING FOR OTHERS

OVER THE YEARS people have asked me to recreate their childhood memories on canvas. The process is not unlike how I went about depicting Roch Carrier's boyhood. I took notes, reviewed old photographs, and visited the actual sites when I could.

For instance, in the mid-1980s, I set about painting Devonshire Elementary School in Montreal. Once a bustling institution in the heart of the old Jewish immigrant district, it was about to be demolished.

The surrounding houses, half a century later, were still standing but, as would be expected, had become very dilapidated. I listened to stories from that neighbourhood by someone who resided there in the 1930s and '40s. A particular anecdote stayed with me. It involved a corner

flat directly across from the school, where one of the local mothers would take in men (so it was rumoured) to make extra money.

If this was true, I wondered whether it might have been the action of a woman — perhaps a widow — desperate to feed her children. In those days, the after-effects of the Depression fell hard on everyone, especially immigrants who had to scrounge for their survival.

But it was scandalous, all the same, and I could imagine the juicy gossip that must have swirled through the community. I pieced together a story for my painting: kids playing up and down the street (then paved in cobblestones), the woman's daughter idly waiting on the balcony (perhaps sent out there while her mother carried on her business inside), and a sailor leaving the house as the woman peers out from behind the curtains (possibly looking for her next customer).

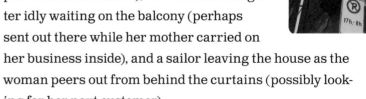

How close is this painting to reality? We'll never know, nor will the two neighbours exchanging malicious whispers on the corner.

ANOTHER PAINTING FROM that era, in the same neighbourhood, was commissioned by the granddaughter of a
shoemaker. He set up shop on Rachel Street. I love the name
of his establishment: Karpman Shoe Hospital. ("The place
for sick soles"—the motto I would have suggested for the
front window—but I'm forty years too late.)

The building was still standing when I went to photograph it and make preliminary sketches. The business no
longer belonged to the family, but I was glad to hear that
the terms of sale included keeping the original name.

When I learned that the grandmother used to bring her
husband a cooked meal from home every day, I decided
that would be the treasured memory for the granddaughter to hang on her wall.

THE SUBJECT OF my next painting was also a grandfather. This elderly man, cherished by the grandson whose wife commissioned the work, spent much of his retirement on the balcony of his apartment building. He was adored by his grandchildren, but to any of the local kids whose baseball ended up on his lawn, look out! He would confiscate the ball and shoo them away.

I decided to make a painting that would affectionately portray that endearing grumpiness found in all of our grandparents. (I must admit, by the end of this painting I felt like I could be Sheldon Rockwell, Norman's long lost Canadian cousin.)

ONE OF MY commissions was of the old Montreal Forum at Sainte-Catherine Street and Atwater — the long-standing home of the Rocket and his Stanley Cup–winning team-mates.

What exactly did it look like before all those modern renovations? I needed the 1960s version, with that famous vertical-hanging sign and old-time marquee.

The person who commissioned the painting was a for-mer policeman whose beat was on that very block. His memory of supervising traffic during Saturday night hockey games outside this landmark was one he wanted me to capture on canvas.

After collecting my usual research, I came up with a rough sketch which he readily approved.

I couldn't wait to show him the finished product. Before bringing it to him, I threw in some last-minute treats that would add to the life of the scene: a local drunk mooching a cigarette from a passerby and a ticket scalper trying to make a fast buck. The storyteller in me loved including details like these, and it would be fun to surprise my policeman patron with them.

Oh, he was surprised, all right.

"What are *they* doing there?" He glared at the painting when I brought it to his house. "I would never let those bums anywhere *near* the Forum!"

Back in my studio, I covered up the unwanted offenders with a thick layer of gesso and repainted the scene. It was like they were never there. The reputation of an ex-cop would remain as clean as a whistle and his public service properly preserved. I was certain to have a happy customer once again. I rinsed out my brush and poured the dirty liquid from my water jar down the paint-splattered drain of my studio sink. All in a day's work!

PAINTING FOR MYSELF

OCCASIONALLY, I WILL seek out subjects based on one simple criterion: a desire to paint whatever calls out to me.

Cows will do it every time. For instance, I fell under the spell of this black and white herd grazing along the banks of Rivière Yamaska outside of Montreal.

Looking at the artwork now, I don't know how I had the patience to paint it. The image could almost be a photograph—but not quite. I do remember applying all the minute details to my canvas—including every blade of grass—without too much thought behind what I was painting. In fact, I was surprised when a friend of mine later remarked, "Oh, look, you painted a pregnant cow."

"I did?"

"That one, with the giant udder."

Holy cow! Who knew?

MONTREAL IS A city with back streets made for artists. One wintry afternoon, I took my camera and sketchbook into the heart of the Plateau region, losing myself in a snow-bound network of wooden sheds and rundown garages.

I knew there was a painting here, if I let the right elements fall into place. I discovered some details directly in front of me, like the steeple and dome of Saint Viateur's Church.

Others came on their own, like a grey-striped cat that jumped out of my imagination and onto the roof of the shed.

A BLANK CANVAS

THESE COMMISSIONS AND personal paintings have been a sideline for me—one that I rarely undertake any more. For the most part, animated films and children's books have consumed my professional life for the past forty years.

The true artist needs to stay open, ready to be pointed in new directions at any time. For me, the time is now. I find myself switching gears these days and following fresh creative outlets using my art.

Before moving on, however, I want to sign off with my final illustration from my last children's book, *Kishka for Koppel* (Orca Book Publishers, 2011), written by Toronto storyteller Aubrey Davis.

Kishka for Koppel was adapted from an animated short I directed in 2008, called *The Three Wishes*. The film wasn't successful in any commercial way and received no major recognition. But the story's message could not have spoken louder to me: Forget smash hits, forget awards. There are treasures right in front of us all the time—in the ordinary life we live, in the everyday world we wake up to. Here is where the artist thrives.

I'm thrilled to have been able to share my creative journey, thus far, with you.

I wish you well on your own path, wherever that finds you right now—with the magic always close at hand.

EPILOGUE

A LIFE OF ITS OWN

TWO SIDES OF THE SWEATER

THE REFLECTIONS AND insights expressed in this book extend beyond my personal work. They involve universal principles that apply to my own creativity as much as to yours.

I would like to conclude, therefore, by recognizing two more "truths" I've uncovered while working on my projects—and like all truths, they each have their own paradox. I mention them now because I believe they can open the way for all of us who struggle to make something out of nothing... and what better way to close a book than with an opening?

The work is not easy. Animators, in particular, know just how much time and effort it takes to get to *The End*. I used to complain about the intensity of making *The Sweater* until *Snow Cat* crept into the picture and took five times longer to complete. When the stress level became unbearable, I would look back longingly at *The Sweater* and think what a breeze it was to make that film.

How do we get through it? We only need to listen to the Rocket, himself, for the simplest advice on reaching our goals: *never give up.*

This is the parting message that Maurice Richard left behind. Fans will discover those words of inspiration inscribed on his tombstone below a solid bronze impression of his handprint—a powerful symbol of the physical in life: reaching out, and doing, and holding on tenaciously.

And to this I add the accompanying paradox: As we hold on, we must also let go. Whatever goals we strive for, whatever tasks we undertake with relentless effort—these can only be achieved successfully by giving ourselves over to something beyond us: the physical and the spiritual in partnership, neither enough by itself.

The Sweater arrived out of nowhere, like a gift ready to be wrapped in ten thousand sheets of animation paper. It is worth noting that the magic appeared first, and the work followed, which leads me to another truth when it comes to creating—the one I believe that is most important of all: We need a spark to set everything in motion. Something inside of us must be ignited: our own personal pilot light.

Without that individual passion propelling the artist forward, there will be no motivation to sustain the effort. We require this drive to burn inside of us in order to see our visions manifest. From that standpoint, creation is primarily an inner, selfish act.

And the paradox: Self-creating must ultimately be for others or there can be no true fulfillment. It is never enough to do things for oneself. The true reward is in the gift.

And now that it is out of my hands, there seems to be no limit to the ways in which you have taken this sweater and made it your own.

This sweater is for you!

BREAK

AWAY!

ACROSS CANADA

ONE OF MY favourite anecdotes about *The Hockey Sweater* is told by Montreal *Gazette* journalist Bernie Goedhart, who discovered two unexpected spokesmen for the story while she was travelling out west in the earlier days of her career. She writes:

I've long loved The Hockey Sweater, *and routinely give it as a gift to people with children, or to people who live outside Canada. Whenever possible, I try to combine it with a DVD of the National Film Board version because I love the animation and especially enjoy the sound of Roch Carrier's voice.*

Sometimes I forget, though, that I'm not alone in my passion for this Canadian icon.

Many years ago, while working for Via Rail as editor of their employee newspaper, I was on board the Skeena, a train that runs from Jasper, Alberta, to Prince Rupert in northern British Columbia. It was after midnight; other passengers had retired for the night and I was the only one left in the club car, talking with the conductor while he did paperwork. It was all very peaceful, and I was learning a lot about the train and its clientele, when the door suddenly opened and a burly, bearded man came in.

He greeted the conductor like an old friend, and threw me a look as if to say What's she doing in here? *When he heard that I worked at VIA headquarters in Montreal, the look was even more disdainful. (Turns out this man was a CN locomotive engineer; headquarter types spelled office workers and/or management—a definite step down, in his eyes, from onboard personnel.) He softened some when the conductor told him that I also wrote for a newspaper, reviewing children's literature. "Oh yeah?" he said. "Ever meet that guy who wrote* The Hockey Sweater? *Roch Carrier? I love that book. Used to listen to him tell the story on cbc at Christmas. Now I read the book with my kids." He turned to the conductor and asked if he'd ever heard of it, and when the conductor responded by reciting the first couple of lines of the story, the engineer grinned and joined in.*

They alternated, first one, then the other, until they'd recited most of the text. What's more, they did it in Roch Carrier's voice, with his Québécois accent!

I couldn't believe it. Two Westerners. Two anglophones. One of them a large, gruff, tattooed locomotive engineer. Reciting, off by heart, the text of The Hockey Sweater *in a French-Canadian accent. Without a hint of irony or mockery. Just joyfully, enthusiastically, as homage.*

It was a defining moment for me, riding that train through northern B.C. in the dead of night, with two Canadian trainmen who loved the book as much as I did.

ACROSS THE BORDER

A NUMBER OF years ago, Tundra Books passed along a copy of an Australian journal that came their way, entitled *Papers: Exploring Children's Literature*. The lead article was written by Dr. Anne Hiebert Alton, a Canadian Professor of English teaching at Central Michigan University in the United States. She very skilfully constructed a multi-layered analysis of *The Hockey Sweater*, subtitling her piece, "A Canadian Cross-Cultural Icon."

In addition to exploring historical, political, and social insight into the story — which opened my eyes to aspects that I had never seen before — she included references to my creative input. I felt she genuinely understood the process I undertook in my artwork and critiqued it in a very informative and complimentary context. I wanted to thank her and did just that in a short email.

I include her reply here because she expressed to me personally (as much as she did academically in her article) how deeply the story has woven its way into the fabric of our Canadian identity.

Dear Sheldon,

Thank you so much for your email regarding my article on *The Hockey Sweater*. I'm so delighted to hear from you! It means a lot to me (and this is very much an understatement) that you think I did a good job of analysing the story and your accompanying animation and illustrations to it.

I hope that my article was able to express just how significant the story has been for me, as I'm sure it has been for a number of other Canadians: that story and your illustrations really express in a nutshell many of the implications of what it means to be Canadian, and I say this as a Canadian who has lived away from home for a decade. Funnily enough, I've discovered that I often feel more Canadian now than I did before we left: there's nothing like contrast, particularly that of another culture, to remind you of who you are.

I'm looking forward to showing my son, who was born a few years ago, the video and reading him the book, and thus indoctrinating him in some of his cultural heritage; he's already interested in speaking French, which I'm delighted about, and last year he took to announcing that he lived in "Mount Pleasant, Canada" (he watches Kids CBC in the mornings). In any case, I hope that he too will enjoy the story and perhaps begin to identify with, or at the very least understand, some of the contradictions that define Canada.

I must tell you that the first time my husband, an Australian by birth but who lived in Canada for seven years, saw the film (we were living in Toronto at the time) his first response was to say, "That's exactly what Canada is, isn't it!" So you see, the story really does cross cultural boundaries.

Many, many thanks for taking the time to write, and of course also for animating and illustrating the work in the first place.

Cheers,

Anne

ACROSS THE OCEAN

SOMEWHERE INSIDE THE great expanse of Buckingham Palace, perhaps in one of the rooms that was set aside for Prince William as a boy, a copy of *The Hockey Sweater* may very well be resting on a bookshelf. In 1991, it was presented to Prince Charles and Princess Diana as one of the official gifts for their young sons during a Royal visit to Canada.

Could it be that the glossy cover of this children's book is still being dusted off on a regular basis by a contingent of dutiful chambermaids? I like to think at some point there was a dignified remark of "Terribly amusing!" from the Queen herself as she came across the antics of young Roch with his brand new hockey sweater.

AND FROM ENGLAND, the story continues to travel down the map, past the equator . . .

"I just returned from Africa," my family doctor told me during a recent checkup in her office. "I could hardly believe my eyes," she said, folding her stethoscope at the end of the examination. "There was your book, displayed in one of the store windows in Victoria Falls!"

Apparently, images of the snowy village of Sainte-Justine can be found on the pages of *The Hockey Sweater* in the unlikely setting of another little town, this one blazing under the African sun.

ANOTHER EXAMPLE OF this homespun tale catching the attention of readers and viewers around the globe comes from Germany. For its Christmas edition, the Munich newspaper *Süddeutsche Zeitung* devoted the entire front page of its sports section to *The Hockey Sweater* and Roch Carrier. I imagined subscribers setting off for last-minute holiday shopping starting their day with a hot cup of "kaffee" and an inviting glimpse into snowy "Kanada."

Translation of title and subtitle:

Playing in the Winterland
*Roch Carrier from Sainte-Justine does not need
many words to explain Canada — he just tells
the story of his hockey sweater.*

I had the opportunity to meet the young German sports editor, Thomas Hahn, who wrote this wonderful article. He had arranged a special trip to Montreal on his own time so that he could visit Sainte-Justine with Roch Carrier, just as I had done thirty years before when I collected my own research.

Süddeutsche Zeitung   SPORT   Freitag, 24. Dezember 2010
Bayern Seite 41

Spielen im Winterland

Roch Carrier aus Sainte-Justine braucht nicht viele Worte, um Kanada zu erklären – er erzählt einfach die Geschichte von seinem Eishockey-Sweater

Sie ließen ihn nicht mitspielen, weil er das Toronto-Trikot trug.

„Keiner hat mir so viel gesagt wie Maurice Richard."

Die Jugend hat heute mehr vom Eis als nur die Fläche fürs Spiel.

Thomas was fascinated with our country's passion for hockey and the place of prominence it holds in our culture. Then he came across Roch's short story and became particularly enamoured with it. I was curious how he discovered this childhood tale and asked him if he would contribute a brief explanation for my own book. I didn't expect the poignancy of his answer.

I first learned about The Hockey Sweater *during the Olympic Games in Vancouver. Or to be exact: I learned about its opening lines. I noticed that there were hockey kids on the back of the Canadian five-dollar bill and some words next to it in English and French. I liked it, and I thought about the fact that soccer, Germany's game, would never make it on a money bill. Soccer is important in Germany, but I often feel its cultural value is underestimated.*

I discovered more about The Hockey Sweater *just prior to the Olympic hockey final with Canada vs. USA. There was an article in the* New York Times *about Canada's game and it mentioned that the words on the Canadian five-dollar bill were from a story by Roch Carrier.*

After the Olympics I spent some more time in Vancouver and looked out for the book. I expected a novel or at least an epic short story and was surprised when I saw that The Hockey Sweater, *obviously the defining story about a hockey childhood in Canada, was a kids' book.*

Then I read it and it really touched me. Its simple words, its simple images. Its power without being powerful. Its political content without being political.

I decided to bring it to Germany and to write about it. And so I did and at home it seemed that everyone who got in touch with the book was enchanted by the words and the images of it — just as I had been.

And I felt, this is how we need to find orientation in this complex world and to overcome the barriers between us: a few words from the heart and some colour, nothing more.

Thomas Hahn

ACROSS THE STRATOSPHERE

IN THE FINAL sequel of *The Hockey Sweater* series, entitled *The Basketball Player*, I designed an end-leaf displaying all of the favourite books the author read as a child: works by Jules Verne, Mark Twain, Villon, Rimbaud, Hans Christian Anderson — writers and poets who inspired him from a very early age.

However, I learned that one of Roch's biggest treats in those days was not a book at all, but a comic. He told me how he loved to read the latest space adventures of Brick Bradford. Therefore I included one of his comic books in the illustration, featuring a "futuristic" 1940s version of a rocket ship blasting through outer space.

If you imagine young Roch glued to these intergalactic exploits, it becomes all the more meaningful when I conclude with this most incredible email that Roch received just as I was nearing the completion of this book.

```
Date: November 16, 2010 2:51:54 PM EST (CA)
From: Thirsk, Robert B. (jsc-cb)[canadian space agency]
To: Roch Carrier
Subject: Your Book in Space
```
Bonjour M. Carrier. I am Canadian astronaut Robert Thirsk. I had the privilege last year to fly aboard the International Space Station for six months. This spaceflight was a personal thrill and the highlight of my professional career.

I had the opportunity to fly a small number of personal objects in space with me. Since astronauts are advocates for literacy, I chose to fly a copy of your book *Le Chandail de Hockey*. This book is a classic within our national culture and you are a great Canadian author. I would be pleased to present this book to you, if you would like to have it. Meilleurs voeux.

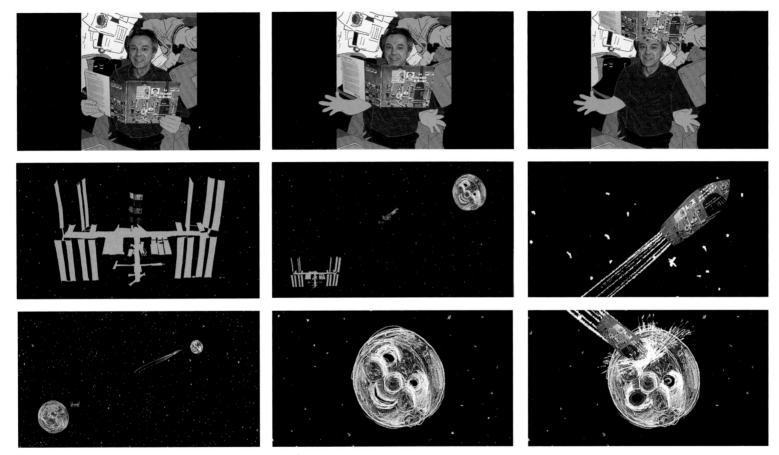

THIS IS A STORYBOARD I created for Rhombus Media, under the direction of Barbara Willis-Sweete. Her film documents how far and wide *The Hockey Sweater* has travelled recently, highlighting its latest journey through the concert hall of the Toronto Symphony Orchestra in a special musical adaptation of the story . . . and including astronaut Robert Thirsk's launching of the book into space!

A NOTE BEFORE Roch Carrier's afterword...

More than once, I've been with other artists who boasted of receiving "such a beautiful letter of rejection" from this committee or that publisher. I myself have been known to say "Wow, I'm so honoured. You wouldn't believe who personally turned me down!"

My most cherished rejection to date, however, comes from the members of the Endowments and Prizes Section of the Canada Council for the Arts. The reason I treasure this event so much, even thought my nomination for the Artistic Achievement Award fell on deaf ears, was because the application itself produced an incredible letter of recommendation from Roch Carrier.

When it came time for the publisher of this book to contact Roch to write an afterword about my artwork and our collaboration, I told my editor, "Don't bother, I already have it in the top drawer of my desk." That's where I keep Roch's letter of recommendation. It'll be there until they pry the paintbrush from my hand and cart me away. The truth is, even though the creative process ought to be an egoless endeavour, we all need personal affirmation for what we do. So, thank you, Roch, for finally getting me that letter of recommendation I never received from the animation instructor at Sheridan College.

AFTERWORD BY ROCH CARRIER

In the form of a letter to the Canada Council for the Arts, submitted a number of years ago

Dear Officer,

It gives me great pleasure to nominate Mr. Sheldon Cohen as a candidate for the prestigious Governor General Awards in Visual and Media Arts 2008 in the category "Artistic Achievement Award" and to support his candidacy. Mr. Cohen has a life dedicated to his art; his contribution to the medium is most impressive; he never ceased to grow in it and to push it forward. As the true great artist, he is quietly modest about his accomplishments because he is much more interested in the new experience that challenges him than by what he already created, however impressive it is. His talent has already been recognized by a significant number of international organizations, as well as Canadian ones, such as the Governor General Literary Award for Book Illustration. Such recognition can be confirmed, if necessary, by the numerous people of all ages, all generations, all backgrounds who were touched by his books or his films. One of the books he illustrated sold over 250,000 copies; his drawings have made, and are making, the story accessible to all; and many see that story through Sheldon's drawing. The same could be said about the film

he created from that story. It's safe to say that *The Sweater* has been seen by some millions of people, in many countries, in many schools, theatres, planes, classrooms, for all kinds of objectives: seeing a story, learning languages, selling popcorn, promoting Canada, immigration or tourism, etc.... All that happened because Sheldon created an inspired and inspiring work of art. And what he did more than twenty years ago seems to be as fresh as it was when he did it.

I had the privilege of seeing the artist at work. First, there was a research phase. Sheldon is very serious about learning what he will be talking about. He was searching like an historian. Then came an intriguing phase; Sheldon appropriated that information and started using it for its purpose; it was most fascinating to watch that information used as a matter to be shaped in some way that it would reach another level.

I witnessed him working on animated films: to express what he is doing, he never used the jargon preferred by many artists; his inventive strength is not in the abstract theory. It's in the real doing. It's beautiful to listen to him explaining to fascinated kids how you illustrate a book or how you draw a film. Sheldon never forgets the story he is telling, but he is always looking for the best way to say it with his drawings. He is looking for an unexpected perspective, an astonishing sequence of moves, diverse points of view; he stresses the importance of the object in his drawing according to the life it takes in the story. And he makes all kinds of choices that are magic for me; as an artist, Sheldon makes them through creative logic and intuitive reason.

It is also fascinating to see how Sheldon imports to a medium ways of another medium. First, it should be said that he knows perfectly well the essence of a book and of a film. But through them, Sheldon migrated techniques from one to the other. His books are not static, they move like film: The visual aspects of his films, its visual linguistics, are coherent, encompassed, constructed in some way where you can read them like a book which would have a greater power. In my mind, it is a great quality.

I don't feel like I'm doing a great job in trying to explain why Sheldon Cohen should be recognized for his high qual-ity body of work in the field of book illustration and film animation. I feel sorry that some of the writers he collaborated with or whose work he illustrated are not here to do what I'm trying to do: how great an artistic adventure it has been to share a creative experience with such a modest man who is such a great artist who transforms the reality before your eyes to better express it.

His work has been accomplished over a period of more than thirty years. He could have been satisfied with what has been done and use the formula for the next project. It was not Sheldon's way. With some kind of serenity, and some amount of assurance of his capacities, this artist is inhabited by a doubt: is what he did the best he can do? With the satisfaction of having done a good job — which he did — he goes back to his work with the conviction that he can improve it. And he can. This mix of anxiety about his project and of assurance that he can do it through hard work and listening to his intuition endow his work with solidity, a depth that makes it durable as time goes on. In his drawings, in books as in films, there is a moving freshness that sticks with you. It could be the essence of his style.

I must confess that it is not easy to write words about this great and modest artist (I repeat those words) when what I know best, after a long and durable partnership, is how patient a worker he is, moving from draft to draft, adding new ideas, thinking of a new technique, of a new angle; using for the books camera moves, angles, techniques that he borrows from the art of filming. Sometimes also, he takes from the illustrated books techniques he applies to his films, giving them new possibilities. The extent of his pictorial vocabulary and syntax is wide and rich. He accepts the story, he respects the story; the story, in his view does not impose limitations for him but he uses it as a springboard to jump higher, bringing the story with him. Doing so, Sheldon created his art and the writer thinks: this is my story, but better.

I don't think I express myself correctly, trying to support Sheldon Cohen's candidacy. In his films, like in his books, he created a highly innovative style and, at the same time, he makes them easy to connect with. His drawings are complex but everyone is seduced by their simplicity. If anybody needs to be convinced, please, just open *The Fly-ing Canoe*. Sheldon is always faithful to the principles of his art, whatever the era of the story. In that adaptability, he remains true to himself and he added truth to the story by the seriousness of his research and the invention he transformed it with.

The organizations that recognized in the past Sheldon's art would be able, I imagine, to support what I'm trying to say. Communication-Jeunesse, the American Institute of Graphics, the juries of the Governor General Awards would probably have better words. IBBY too. In his great modesty, Sheldon mentions that award among those he received. He should have said that IBBY is the great and big international institution representing from all over the world those involved in the field of books for young readers. These people noticed Sheldon Cohen's work. I suppose they know what they do.

To conclude, I will say that when Sheldon asked me if I would accept to nominate him as a candidate to the most prestigious Governor General Awards in Visual and Media Arts 2008 (Artistic Achievement Award) I thought within myself that it is an honour for me. And I'm doing it with my sincerity. I might lack the words to support his file but I know at least one thing, and it is very important to me: With his illustrations in books and films Sheldon brought to reading hundreds of thousands of kids. On top of that, he probably inspired as many kids to take pencils and draw. This also is quite an accomplishment! And I am not mentioning the numerous artists who admire and study his books and films and try to understand what makes it work.

Now, it is to the members of the jury to decide. Please, just forget what I wrote and see the books, watch the films! And I wish you all to have an opportunity to meet this modest great artist and just talk with him about what he does.

Sincerely,

Roch Carrier

END CREDITS

I AM VERY fortunate to have had the opportunity of animating films at the National Film Board of Canada. Few places in the world encourage director-driven projects such as *The Sweater*, while at the same time providing the most skilled production crews possible. *The Sweater* team could not have been better.

A few names I'd like to highlight . . .

Celebrated composer Normand Roger: From those very first chords over the NFB logo, his music sweeps us into the film, carrying us from one scene to the next. The melody Normand used was based on 1940s sensation La Bolduc, who belted out songs in a lively celebration of her Québécois roots.

THE COLOURING TEAM: Zina Heczko, Françoise Hartman, and supervisor Eunice Macaulay, the "mother hen" of the animation studio, who took the arduous *trace-and-paint* responsibilities under her wing and always made our production feel it was doing just fine, regardless of the pressure. I'm so glad to have had the finesse of these "old-school" artists who applied their skills in the vital way that computers could never accomplish now.

CO-PRODUCER AND PICTURE editor David Verrall: He is mostly recognized for his long-standing executive producer role at the NFB animation studio. But I wonder if people know of the superb hands-on contribution he made to *The Sweater*.

Aside from supervising the entire production, David taught me the utter importance of fine-cutting a movie. Through his incredible precision of removing a few frames here and a few frames there, I became acutely aware of how important it was to keep the right flow of storytelling from scene to scene. His participation on *The Sweater* was invaluable and impacted the way I made films ever since. I am very grateful for his influence.

CO-PRODUCER Marrin Canell: This great producer's love for the project was equalled only by his determination to see it off the ground. I consider him to be at the very core of this production and credit him for igniting the original spark that led to all the rest. If there were to be a chronological order assigned to the film crew, Marrin would be first on the list. Whenever I think of *The Sweater* and how it came to be, I see it as "Marrin's film." In fact, when he first pitched the story to the NFB, it was suggested the project be developed as a live-action drama. "No way," said Marrin. "This is animation!" The rest is history

ADDITIONAL THANKS TO Wolf Koenig and Derek Lamb for their background support as executive producers.

HERE ARE THE complete credits as they appear at the end of the film. My sincere gratitude goes out to all of these very talented coworkers who helped piece the movie together with the unique contribution each of them made.

The Sweater
Produced by the National Film Board of Canada
Director and Animator: Sheldon Cohen
Writer and Narrator: Roch Carrier
Sound and Music: Normand Roger
Assistant Animator: Robert Doucet
Colourists: Zina Heczko, Eunice Macaulay,
 Françoise Hartman
Animation Camera: Jacques Avoine, Raymond Dumas,
 Richard Moras, Pierre Landry
Consultant: Gerald Budner
Editor: David Verrall
Hockey Commentary: Jean-Guy Moreau
English Text: Sheila Fischman
Sound Recording: Roger Lamoureux
Music Recording: Louis Hone
Post-Sync Effects: Ken Page, C.F.E.
Re-recording: Jean-Pierre Joutel
Unit Administrator: Diane Bergeron
Producers: Marrin Canell, David Verrall
Executive Producer: Derek Lamb

A NOTE ON the technique used in *The Sweater*:

Traditional animation with a bit of twist! The characters were traced onto frosted cels (not the usual clear acetates), which allowed each figure to be shaded with coloured pencils — a technique, for instance, that you would never see in a standard Disney movie at that time. The reason large commercial studios painted their cels "flat" was because any sketchy quality applied to the characters (such as shading with coloured pencils) would *boil* on screen. It is impossible to match all those pencil lines from frame to frame and therefore they will flicker like mad when the film is run through the projector, hence the term *boiling*.

"It's messy. It looks unfinished, like a child did it. Clean it up!" This is what most producers in commercial studios would have said about the animation of *The Sweater* if it were made anywhere else but at the NFB.

My producers, on the other hand, said, "Go for it!" and allowed me to boil and flicker as much as I wanted.

There was one problem, however, with this technique. The animation "went dead" when the movement stopped. Therefore, I used a trick of the trade that another NFB animator taught me: tracing three drawings for the same "held" position and alternating them at random: A, B, C; B, C, A; C, A, B. In this way, when characters were static they continued to "breathe" — perhaps looking messy and unfinished — but always alive!

I took a different approach for the opening and closing scenes, when the sled animates through the snow: oil pastels smeared with turpentine directly on paper. This provided a more flowing effect to the animation so you could feel yourself travelling through space coming into and out of the village.

The same oil pastels were applied to my "backgrounds" throughout the film. Therefore, even when the cel-painted characters appeared on screen, I was able to maintain a sense of visual continuity in the overall rendering.

I don't remember making an intentional choice to go with this painterly look. I simply followed the style that came most naturally to me. It's almost like the animation had to fit into my art rather than the other way around. The result is a technique that doesn't quite belong to one particular category.

IN THE EARLY 1980s, the NFB Animation Department encouraged world-renowned animator Caroline Leaf to try her hand at producing. When she showed me "Pies" by author Wilma Riley, I jumped at the chance to direct this short story under her supervision.

We immediately set about creating a screenplay for the film. Collaborating with someone as gifted as Caroline was an enriching experience I will always treasure — especially remembering the great fun we had working together.

The animation technique for *Pies,* unlike *The Sweater*, was based on a very deliberate choice on my part to stylize the look of the film in a very specific way. I wanted the design to be bold and punchy, so that the artwork would properly reflect the colourful storyline.

Much of the shooting was on "3s" (triple-framing the drawings) to create exaggerated movement. The backgrounds and characters were rendered in brilliant hues, carefully selected by talented artist Elaine Gasco. It was mesmerizing to watch her. With the concentration of a scientist, she mixed and matched and stirred and poured every colour of cel paint possible, using wooden coffee stir-sticks to fill dozens and dozens of empty baby food jars (the animator's equivalent of stirring rods and test tubes). She and her team also painstakingly outlined every image in the film with a fine-tipped nib pen — a throwback to the early days of animation.

When Ontario composer Alex Pauk (who later became a renowned musical director and conductor) added his richly flavoured music score into the mix, all the spice I wanted for this film had come together.

FOR *SNOW CAT*

AFTER AWARD-WINNING CHILDREN'S book author and illustrator Dayal Kaur Khalsa was diagnosed with cancer, she devoted all of her time to creating joyful and humorous stories, in spite of the struggle she faced.

One story that stood out from the rest, because of its subject matter, was her haunting legend *Snow Cat* about healing the wounds of loss. I bought the rights to this mythological tale and assembled a storyboard to pitch as a short film, which later evolved into a half-hour TV special.

With the eventual collaboration of NFB producer Marcy Page and independent producer Kenneth Hirsch (two of the sharpest minds in the industry, and the most decent of human beings to boot), I formed a film crew headed by animator Jeami (short for Jean-Michel) Labrosse. Working out of a rustic studio deep in the country, he was the perfect candidate to bring my storyboard of *Snow Cat* to life. A brilliant animator, he invented an experimental

fingerpaint technique, which he applied on a specially designed camera stand in his attic.

The entire film was animated on a children's toy called "The Fingerpainter." Jeami pulled apart the components of this toy, separating out a viscous graphite medium that remained hermetically sealed between two pieces of acetate (ideally designed for obsessively clean parents who wanted creative children, just not messy ones).

Using these acetates as his background palette, he underlit the liquified graphite that was sealed inside them. This gave a glowing effect to the images he created. There were no pencils or paper involved—just his fingers "shmooshing the goo" (as I like to call it) to create the animation. I realize I am not providing the most sophisticated description to impress you with how this movie was made, but imagine what it would be like to single-handedly animate a half-hour film on an Etch A Sketch—that's the equivalent of what Jeami did in his tiny attic in the country!

Once the animation was completed, each of the thousands of frames was hand-painted directly on the 35mm film itself using a watercolour technique developed by Brazilian animator Daniel Schorr.

During the final step when the film was being processed in the NFB lab, I remember being lulled by the rhythmic beats of the optical printer, which cranked out one painted frame after another. It was not unlike the feeling I would get when travelling by train and listening to the clicking of the wheels against the tracks. There was something very comforting as I watched the last few frames wind around the film core. It had taken me more than ten years to get to this point in my *Snow Cat* journey. Only one element was missing now: the music. It is here that the emotions of a story are expressed where words and images fall short. Therefore, the soundtrack of a movie is as important to me as the picture.

I already had Maureen Stapleton's masterful narration, and I wanted an equally powerful music track. Once again, I relied on the expertise of composer Normand Roger. He created a highly textured and sensitive score that filled out the visuals with the perfect atmosphere.

An additional song, "Dreams Come True," was written especially for the DVD release by Montreal songwriter Linda Morrison. One of my favourite moments in the film is the happy-go-lucky sequence of the two main characters playing in the snow, set to Linda's beautiful song.

"When dreams come true, you get on board and ride them. Make your dreams come true, travelling on inside them . . ."

THE AUTHOR PASSED away without ever seeing the movie completed, but, like the message of *Snow Cat*, Dayal remains with us even though she's gone. A part of her will always be lovingly held inside the many stories she left behind.

FOR *I WANT A DOG*

IT WAS ANOTHER of Dayal's books that inspired my next movie.

Because her artwork is similar in style to mine, the transition from book to film was a smooth one, especially with the help of digital expert Jon Gasco. He skilfully re-rendered my hand-drawn backgrounds on his computer as if Dayal herself had painted them. This was my goal. I wanted the art in the film to reflect the utter brilliance of Dayal's illustrations so that the images on screen would seem to have been animated right off the pages of her picture book. I don't know how he did it, but incredibly, Jon was able to do just that, using only a stylus and tablet to recreate her art from scratch. I thoroughly understoond why "expert" followed "digital" in his job description.

As in all areas of life, computers had become an intrinsic part of the animation process by this time and there was no turning back. Inking and painting were now obsolete, replaced with software that could do in minutes what might have taken weeks in my *Sweater* days. Yes, it was a new and speedier world, but it brought with it a corresponding fresh set of challenges that, in the end, kept the process just as

intricate and complex — perhaps even more so — and somehow equally time-consuming.

I personally don't see the essence of animation having changed with the advent of this new technology, including the growing popularity of 3D movies. The audience will always walk away empty if the animator doesn't put his or her heart and soul into the work, no matter how much technical pizzazz is offered otherwise.

Having said that, I'm extremely grateful to the NFB for providing access to some of its abundant pizzazz offered by truly wonderful tech support.

I relied on the same basic foundation for *I Want a Dog* as I did for all my projects: simply wanting to tell the best story I could. In order to do that, I built up a team headed by animator Jo Meuris who assisted me superbly in bringing Dayal's 1950s suburban world to life. Whenever you see a section in the film and think to yourself "Wow, look at the sophistication of that animation!" that would be Jo's work. And then, out of nowhere, when a primitive style suddenly animates by, well, that's me. I'm the first to say that Jo has made me look good in this project. I can't thank her enough for her contribution, along with the other excellent animators who added choice bits throughout the film.

As for the audio track, Toronto actress Marnie McPhail provided a very charming narration — totally whimsical — playing all the parts herself.

A doo-wop music score by versatile composer Zander Ary was tailor-made to accompany Marnie's voice-over. Zander is a big reason why the film was so much fun to make — not only because of his incredible talent, but also because of the enthusiasm and humour he instilled in the project. He would call me up and say, "I found the perfect dog barks we need!" and then play a canine version of Strauss's classic "Blue Danube" over the phone.

Zander also arranged the music for the gifted vocals of singer Neko Case. Although Neko's usual indie style is rooted in folk and alternative music, she wasn't fazed in the least at the prospect of working on a children's film.

I had no idea how she would react when I first approached her, but when I finally found out how to reach the singer and told her about the project, she instantly agreed. "I love *The Sweater* and I love dogs. I'll do it!"

Her rendition of the title song, written by Penny Will and of Zander Ary's R&B parody, "Walkin' My Rollerskate," infuses an indelible magic into the entire film, marking the soundtrack in a way that no other vocals could.

I give Zander all the credit for directing the final music session. He worked with sound engineer Geoffrey Mitchell, a wizard at the controls, who supervised many of my NFB projects in the past.

For the most part, I sat behind the glass wall of the soundproof booth, not having much to do but listen to Neko deliver one mesmerizing take after another. There was a clear, effortless quality to her voice that carried the listener through the melody.

It makes me wonder now, what in the world was I thinking when I added my two cents out of nowhere:

"Neko, can you try a version with a kind of Ethel Merman ending?"

Ethel Merman? I can't believe I actually said that! I don't know what possessed me, but I wanted her to try belting out the ending of the song.

Thank God people were talking when I made my request and I don't think they heard me. At least, they pretended not to. No one responded.

I knew I'd do best just staying quiet. I slunk back into my chair and let myself be a spectator. Neko and Zander knew exactly what to do. I watched Geoff in front of his giant audio console, masterminding what appeared to be thousands of switches and knobs, like he was at the helm of the *Starship Enterprise*. I took it all in. What an amazing profession I was part of! I felt so fortunate. ("Hey, Neko, how about a round of 'There's *no* business like *show* business!'")

FOR THIS AND THAT

WRITING THIS BOOK offers me the chance to express gratitude that I would otherwise keep to myself, never really saying it to the people I feel it for.

Therefore, I'm taking this opportunity to send out the following public thank-yous (alphabetically):

To Elaine Gasco, the artist who participated in many of the productions I directed. She is also my cousin — the one that got me "Learning to Draw with Jon Gnagy" when we were kids and I'm still at it.

To Kenneth Hirsch, a great producer with his own independent film company, PMA Productions: You're a great friend. I don't know how to thank you for saving the day on many a project! Any director who works with you couldn't ask for more.

To Caroline Leaf, masterful storyteller: No one's art inspires me more than yours.

To Catherine Mitchell: I can't imagine Tundra Books without you behind the scenes, the caring friend of so many authors and artists.

To Marcy Page, NFB producer: An animator's dream! What a privilege to have worked with you!

To Lynn Smith, a pioneer in animation who makes fabulous films: You see the world through artist's eyes and stay true to your vision in a more devoted way than anyone I know. Your friendship means a lot.

To other colleagues whose skills have contributed to my projects in a considerable way: Luigi Allemano (animation assistance, sound work); Giselle Guilbault (administration and budgeting); Greg Houston (co-directing, animating, and DVD authoring); Mike Pelland (computer assistance); and Itsik Romano (digital imaging).

To general supporters over the years, in one way or another: Ruth and David Daniels; Jeannie and Maxie Kirsh; the Kostin-Cohen clan; Eta Yacowar Levi; Sharron Mirsky; Carol Silverman; Sheri Tritt; and Lucy and Nathan Yacowar.

And to some that defy categories: Alexis Johnson, whose genuine goodwill remains to this day.

The late Ricky Rosenbaum, my Buddha-like accountant: You provided refuge to so many struggling artists who had fame and often, very little fortune. I hope you know how much you were appreciated and are smiling down from the other side.

To Murray's Restaurant in the TMR Shopping Centre (it doesn't exist anymore): Sitting at your counter, reading a good book and eating your daily specials — there was nothing like those mid-day breaks to relieve the stress of an animated production.

And finally . . .

To the Moose of La Mancha, the unsung hero of my last animated project — the little film that no one wanted: You inspire me — the way you keep on singing even when they block their ears!

FOR THIS BOOK
A NOD OF thanks to Diane Forestell for planting a seed for this project way back in Abu Dhabi, and to Kerry-Ann Cannon for the thoughtfulness to suggest I submit my manuscript to ECW Press (a very excellent whim on your part, I must say!).

TO THE FOLKS at ECW PRESS . . . three in particular:

David Caron (co-publisher along with Jack David) to whom I will be eternally grateful for saying "Put more of you in the book" when everyone else said, "Sorry, we're only interested in *The Sweater*."

Rachel Ironstone (art director), the stabilizing fulcrum of this project, balancing all the creative elements with superb insight and practical efficiency into one harmonious work.

Ingrid Paulson (freelance book designer) who demonstrated how her craft is an art unto itself and elevated this book to a place it would never have reached without the brilliance of her innovative vision.

TO TUNDRA BOOKS and the National Film Board of Canada for their kind permission to use the many illustrations and movie stills throughout the book — and to Claude Lord, in particular, for his technical expertise in supplying images from *The Sweater*.

AND TO THE following contributors who generously allowed me to add their own words and stories to mine — many thanks: Anne Hiebert Alton, Bernie Goedhart (along with "Klym" Klymchuck and Doug Small, the two railmen she wrote about), Thomas Hahn, Mark P., and Robert Thirsk.

FOR MY FAMILY

WE ALL HAVE a context that we grow out of:

My late mother, Rachel, who took joy in whatever I did and let me roll up her very elegant Oriental carpet so that I could paint big canvases on her living room floor.

MY LATE FATHER, Kelly, so proud of my work, who blurted out in the middle of a large crowd at the 1980 Ottawa International Animation Film Festival: "I don't care what anyone says, *The Sweater* is by far the best film in this whole damn festival."

I can almost smile now without having to cringe, remembering his outrage when I came in second place. At the time I silently prayed that animator Yuri Norstein was far enough away not to hear my father's rant as the great Russian filmmaker accepted the Grand Prize for his incredible masterpiece, *Tale of Tales*.

David, my brother, who shares with me a colourful world of childhood memories from Van Horne Avenue and who has faithfully stood by this Habs tale from day one in spite of being the biggest Bruins fan. Thank you, big brother.

AND WE ALL have a context that we grow into:

My wonderfully bright son, Matthew, with that great sense of humour. He and *The Hockey Sweater* both emerged in the same momentous year of 1984. Even though my wife would probably disagree, I'd say he was a much easier delivery.

My son knows me just as Dad, not as illustrator or animator, but he did think I had the coolest job in the world watching me sit at my desk drawing pictures all day.

Needless to say, he had the good sense to follow a career in commerce and bring some family balance in the end.

IT MAY SOUND odd, but I can say that *The Sweater* found me a bride. You remember my "*Pinocchio* date" that I wrote about at the beginning of this book? I mentioned that she inspired this animator's life for me way back in 1971, but I didn't tell you the whole story.

After some time as a couple, we split up and went our separate ways. She studied for her education degree and became a teacher, while I followed my animation dreams.

It's interesting to note that my job in New York on *Raggedy Ann and Andy* was with Art Babbitt. Guess what he is famous for — being one of the key animators on *Pinocchio*! When I think of the odds of that . . .

So how did we end up getting married, my wife and I? She saw *The Sweater* playing in a movie theatre in 1980 — in those days they still threw in animated fillers before the main feature. It was almost ten years since we had both sat in a theatre just like that one, watching *Pinocchio* together, and now *my* film was up there on the big screen. She started to cry. (Poor guy, whoever she was with!)

The truth is, one of the main reasons the credits rolled by with *Director* and *Animator* attached to my name was because of what she had said to me so long ago, opening my eyes to animation.

She called the day after seeing *The Sweater* to tell me how much she loved the film. We were married in less than six months. The way I see it, it was very clever on her part. She made sure I would be an animator so that years after we broke up I could make a film that would bring us back together.

Of all the prizes I have received for *The Sweater,* none comes close to the greatest reward the film has brought me: my beautiful wife, Donna. I dedicate this book to her.

213

EXCEPT FOR OUR brief collaborations over the years, our paths rarely intersect. But like everyone else, I have watched the achievements of this celebrated author from afar. Aside from his prize-winning career writing stories for books and stage (and at least one little animated film) he has been appointed to a number of very prestigious government positions.

In 1994 I was proud to say, "I know the head of the Canada Council for the Arts."

And then again in 1999 I was proud to say, "I know the head of the National Library of Canada."

What impresses me most, though, is a work ethic that the author exemplifies. Roch mentioned to me that he wakes up early every morning and writes for at least four hours straight, not allowing any disturbances or distractions.

Since he told me that, there have been many pre-dawn mornings when my alarm clock jars me from a deep sleep. I pull myself out of bed and crawl to my desk with eyes half-shut, repeating, "I'm going to be just like Roch Carrier. I'm going to be just like Roch Carrier. I'm going to be… zzzzzzzz."

Roch Carrier has been the greatest of mentors to me. Words can't express my gratitude for this great man's generosity, his wisdom and, most of all, his belief in me as an artist. My entire path would have been very different without his trust in letting me help to tell his story with my art.

I am certain I speak for us all when I say thank you, Roch, for that fleeting bit of magic you spun from your little village of Sainte-Justine to every corner of our country and beyond.

PHOTO CREDITS

KIND THANKS TO the following organizations and individuals for granting permission to reprint images in this book. All images uncredited in the following pages are from author's own collection.

For more information and to watch the films, visit the National Film Board of Canada online at http://www.nfb.ca/explore-all-directors/sheldon-cohen/.

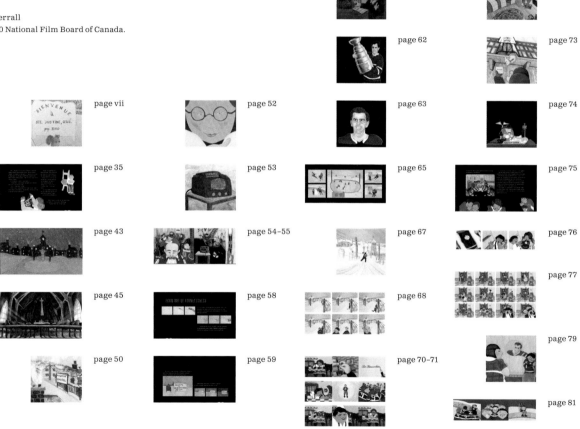

The Sweater, continued . . .

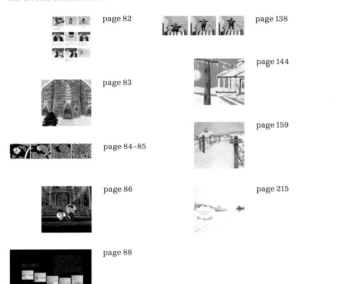

page 82

page 83

page 84–85

page 86

page 88

page 138

page 144

page 159

page 215

Death by Streetcar
Directed by Sheldon Cohen
Produced by Guy Glover
Photo taken from the production © 1977 National Film Board of Canada. All rights reserved.
http://www.nfb.ca/film/poets_on_film_no_2

page 23

Bossa Bop
Directed by Sheldon Cohen
Produced by Wolf Koenig
Photos taken from the production © 1974 National Film Board of Canada. All rights reserved.

page 17

pages 18–19

Pies
Directed by Sheldon Cohen
Produced by Caroline Leaf
Photos taken from the production © 1984, 2004 National Film Board of Canada. All rights reserved.
http://www.nfb.ca/film/pies/

page 94

page 97

page 95

page 98

page 96

page 204

Snow Cat
Directed by Sheldon Cohen
Produced by Sheldon Cohen, Kenneth Hirsch, and Marcy Page
Photo taken from the production © 1998 National Film Board of Canada. All rights reserved.
http://www.nfb.ca/film/snow_cat

 page 102

 page 111

 page 109

 page 206

 page 110

From Book to Film: Animated Classics by Sheldon Cohen
Directed by Sheldon Cohen
Produced by Marcy Page
Photo taken from the production © 2005 National Film Board of Canada. All rights reserved.

 page 15

I Want a Dog
Directed by Sheldon Cohen
Produced by Marcy Page
Photo taken from the production © 2002 National Film Board of Canada. All rights reserved.
http://www.nfb.ca/film/i_want_a_dog

 page 116

 page 125

REPRINTED WITH THE PERMISSION OF TUNDRA BOOKS

The Hockey Sweater, published 1984

 pages 51, 149

 page 141

 page 135

 page 143

 pages 139, 149

The Boxing Champion, published 1991

 page 47

 page 147

 page 145

 pages 148, 149, 150

The Longest Home Run, published 1993

 page 151

 page 152

The Flying Canoe, published 1994

 page 157

 page 158

The Basketball Player, published 1996

 page 153

 page 155

 page 154

I Want a Dog, published 1987

 page 207

OTHER PHOTO NOTES AND CREDITS

Mona Lisa, Leonardo da Vinci. c. 1503–1519. Musée de Louvre, Paris.

page 8

Publicity still from 1935 (public domain).

page 9

Used with permission of the Bank of Canada. Guidelines for reproducing Canadian bank notes can be found at http://www.bankofcanada.ca/banknotes/reproducing-images/.

pages 56–57

Archival photo (public domain).

page 62

Library and Archives Canada, courtesy of Roch Carrier's family (public domain).

page 80

Maureen Stapleton in New York City, 1981. © Walter McBride / Retna Ltd.

page 112

Christine Y. Chiou, *The Harvard Crimson*, May 17, 1999. Copyright © 2011 The Harvard Crimson, Inc. All rights reserved. Reprinted with permission.

page 115

Author's collection. Courtesy of the Cutler family.

page 135

City of Montreal Archives (public domain).

page 167

Courtesy of Orca Book Publishers. From *Kishka for Koppel* (2011) written by Aubrey Davis, illustrated by Sheldon Cohen.

page 175

Copyright Bernie Goedhart.

 page 184   page 185

Author's collection. *Süddeutsche Zeitung Sport Freitag*, page 24. Published December 24, 2010.

 page 189

Used with permission of Rhombus Media. Storyboard from a documentary film being directed by Barbara Willis Sweete, and being produced by Jessica Daniel.

 page 193

By "jmv" at Word on the Street, September 24, 2006, via Wikimedia Commons. Reprinted under a Creative Commons Attribution 2.0 Generic license.

 page 196

Reprinted with permission. Photo by Pierre Obendrauf, The *(Montreal) Gazette*.

 page 223

SHELDON COHEN is an award-winning animator and film director, illustrator, and painter. Specializing in the adaptation of short stories into film, his work includes *The Sweater* (1980), *Pies* (1984), *Snow Cat* (1998), and *I Want a Dog* (2003). He has garnered a long list of international prizes, including the British Academy Award (BAFTA) for Best Animated Film (1981). Having also created artwork for seven picture books, including *The Hockey Sweater* (1984), he received the Governor General's Award for Illustration (1991). Eager to assist students in developing their own film ideas, he has taught animation at Harvard University in Boston and Concordia University in his home town, Montreal, where he currently resides with his wife and son.

ROCH CARRIER was formerly Canada's National Librarian and is the beloved author of many Canadian classics for both adults and children. He has been awarded the Stephen Leacock Award for Humour and several honorary doctorates, and is a Fellow of the Royal Society of Canada and an Officer of the Order of Canada.

A recent photo of Sheldon Cohen (right) and Roch Carrier (left) at Montreal's Bell Centre in front of a sculpture of Maurice "the Rocket" Richard. They were meeting for a promotional event to celebrate their work together — a rewarding collaboration that has spanned over three decades.

At ECW Press, we want you to enjoy this book in whatever format you like, whenever you like. Leave your print book at home and take the eBook to go! Purchase the print edition and receive the eBook free. Just send an email to ebook@ecwpress.com and include:

• the book title
• the name of the store where you purchased it
• your receipt number
• your preference of file type: PDF or ePub?

A real person will respond to your email with your eBook attached. Thank you for supporting an independently owned Canadian publisher with your purchase!

Get the eBook free!